THE LOST STAIRCASE

Elinor M Brent-Dyer

Girls Gone By Publishers

COMPLETE AND UNABRIDGED

Published by
Girls Gone By Publishers, The Vicarage, Church Street, Coleford, Radstock, Somerset, BA3 5NG, UK

First published by W & R Chambers 1946
This edition published 2018
Text © Girls Gone By Publishers
Christmas at the Dragon House © Katherine Bruce 2018
Design and Layout © Girls Gone By Publishers 2018

All rights reserved.
Without limiting the rights under copyright reserved above, no part of this publication may be reproduced, stored in or introduced into a retrieval system, or transmitted, in any form or by any means (electronic, mechanical, photocopying, recording or otherwise), without the prior written permission of the above copyright owners and the above publisher of this book.

Neither Girls Gone By Publishers nor any of their authors or contributors have any responsibility for the continuing accuracy of URLs for external or third-party websites referred to in this book; nor do they guarantee that any content on such websites is, or will remain, accurate or appropriate.

Cover design by Ken Websdale
Typeset in England by Books to Treasure
Printed and bound by Short Run Press, Exeter, EX2 7LW

ISBN 978-1-84745-240-5

'She had swung herself across the sill, and was climbing down the ivy.'—PAGE 203.

CONTENTS

Publishing History	7
Elinor M Brent-Dyer: a Brief Biography	10
The Lost Staircase	13
Christmas at the Dragon House	234
Bibliography	245

PUBLISHING HISTORY

The Lost Staircase was first published in 1946, but Elinor Brent-Dyer had already given the bare outline of the plot in *Lavender Laughs in the Chalet School*, first published in 1943. In the chapter entitled 'The New Seniors' we meet Jesanne Gellibrand and 'her chum', Lois Bennett. Talking to the other seniors, Lois informs them that she has wanted to be curator of a museum '"ever since we found the Lost Staircase"'. The seniors are naturally curious, but Jesanne and Lois do not reveal the whole story since they have decided that they should like the authoress Josephine M Bettany, who they have heard has a connection with the Chalet School, to write it. Very conveniently, Joey arrives at this point, and later Lois and Jesanne go to tea with her. The result was that 'Jo got such a plot for her next book as assured her that she was in for a busy summer'.

Although this was the first of Elinor Brent-Dyer's non-Chalet titles to be advertised in this way, it was not to be the last. The following year, in *Gay from China at the Chalet School*, Gillian Culver is urged by Gay Lambert to tell '"that yarn about the German spy who pretended to be your cousin, and was really a spy"'. In due course the 'yarn' was published as *Chudleigh Hold*.

The first edition of *The Lost Staircase* (1946) was published by W. & R. Chambers and was produced in a wartime-economy format. It was thus thinner than usual, and also smaller in size, being 4¼ x 6¾ inches (approx 11 x 17 cms). The dustwrapper illustration and the black-and-white line frontispiece were by Nina K Brisley (although see the next paragraph). We have used the front of the dustwrapper as our front cover, and have reproduced the spine on the back of our cover; we have also reproduced the frontispiece. The book was reprinted in 1954 in the by then normal

hardback format of 5 x 7½ inches (approx 12½ x 18½ cms). For this edition, the front of the dustwrapper had to have a white border round it in order to make it fit (see left). As far as I know, the book was not reprinted again until the first GGBP edition was published in 2004.

It was only while I was looking at the cover proof for that edition that it occurred to me that the illustration on the spine might not be by Nina K Brisley. The style seems quite unlike hers, and the drawing is not nearly so good—Jesanne looks very stiff, for example. While it was unusual for the Chalet School titles, it was not uncommon at this time for publishers to have one artist for the front of a wrapper and another for the spine.

For this reprint edition, we have included a short story by Katherine Bruce.

Text

For this GGBP edition we have used the original text of the first edition from 1946, which was not altered in subsequent reprints. We have not attempted to correct any editing or author errors, other than typographical ones such as omitted letters and quotation marks; we hope we have not added to them.

Clarissa Cridland

ELINOR M BRENT-DYER: A BRIEF BIOGRAPHY

EBD was born Gladys Eleanor May Dyer in South Shields on 6 April 1894, the only daughter of Eleanor (Nelly) Watson Rutherford and Charles Morris Brent Dyer. Her father had been married before and had a son, Charles Arnold, who was never to live with his father and stepmother. This caused some friction between Elinor's parents, and her father left home when she was three and her younger brother, Henzell, was two. Her father eventually went to live with another woman by whom he had a third son, Morris. Elinor's parents lived in a respectable lower-middle-class area, and the family covered up the departure of her father by saying that her mother had 'lost' her husband.

In 1912 Henzell died of cerebro-spinal fever, another event which was covered up. Friends of Elinor's who knew her after his death were unaware that she had had a brother. Death from illness was, of course, common at this time, and Elinor's familiarity with this is reflected in her books, which abound with motherless heroines.

Elinor was educated privately in South Shields, and returned there to teach after she had been to the City of Leeds Training College. In the early 1920s she adopted the name Elinor Mary Brent-Dyer. She was interested in the theatre, and her first book, *Gerry Goes to School*, published in 1922, was written for the child actress Hazel Bainbridge—mother of the actress Kate O'Mara. In the mid 1920s she also taught at St Helen's, Northwood, Middlesex, at Moreton House School, Dunstable, Bedfordshire, and in Fareham near Portsmouth. She was a keen musician and a practising Christian, converting to Roman Catholicism in 1930, a major step in those days.

In the early 1920s Elinor spent a holiday in the Austrian Tyrol at Pertisau am Achensee, which she was to use so successfully as the first location in the Chalet School series. (Many of the locations in her books were real places.) In 1933 she moved with her mother and stepfather to Hereford, travelling daily to Peterchurch as a governess. After her stepfather died in November 1937 she started her own school in Hereford, The Margaret Roper, which ran from 1938 until 1948. Unlike the Chalet School it was not a huge success and probably would not have survived had it not been for the Second World War. From 1948 Elinor devoted all her time to writing. Her mother died in 1957, and in 1964 Elinor moved to Redhill, Surrey, where she died on 20 September 1969.

Clarissa Cridland

THE LOST STAIRCASE

BY

ELINOR M. BRENT-DYER

CONTENTS

Chap.		Page
I.	The Beginning of it All	17
II.	The Heiress Comes Home	24
III.	The First Tussle	31
IV.	A Truce is Made	39
V.	The House Itself	48
VI.	Enter Miss Mercier!	59
VII.	An Unpleasant Dilemma	75
VIII.	Lessons Begin	88
IX.	Christmas is Coming!	98
X.	The Christmas Season Begins	109
XI.	The Dragon House Ritual	123
XII.	Christmas Day	138
XIII.	A Christmas Surprise	147
XIV.	The Lost Staircase	160
XV.	The First Hint	168
XVI.	'Patience is a Virtue'	177
XVII.	The Search Continues	187
XVIII.	Tommy Lends a Paw	199
XIX.	The Staircase is Found!	207
XX.	Everything Comes Right	215
XXI.	The Last Mysteries Solved	222

TO
MARY
FROM
ELINOR

Chapter I

The Beginning of it All

Dragon House was built during the later years of the Seventh Henry by Master Balthazar Gellibrand. Why Master Gellibrand should have left his native Kent and crossed England to the Welsh Marches to find him a home was a question no one but he could solve. And Master Gellibrand soon became notorious for keeping his mouth tight shut about his private affairs.

He built in the wide, forested plain that spread eastwards from the Welsh Hills, and he built well and truly of grey stone. On the tops of the pillars that marked the boundary walls at intervals were carved great Welsh dragons, and the same device appeared on the gates of twisted iron-work which were brought from Florence, that city of iron-workers. Hence such folk as lived thereabouts—and they were but few—named it the Dragon House; and, the name pleasing Master Gellibrand, the Dragon House it remained.

For two years he dwelt there alone, save for such servants as he hired. Then came a summons to London for the coronation of that king who was to go down to history as wife-murderer and evil-liver. He was away a matter of ten months, and when he returned, he brought with him his bride—a fair-faced girl of sixteen, who was in no awe of her grim dark-browed husband, but filled the house with song and laughter, and ruled as queen of the whole demesne.

For thirty years the pair lived happily together, though the difference in their ages was a score of years. Ten children were born to them, all of whom throve in the soft west-country air, and grew up to comely womanhood and gallant manhood. But when the thirty years ended, Master Balthazar fell sick, and before the week was out they had laid him on his bier.

His widow survived him a bare five months. She fretted and pined for him daily, growing weaker and paler, till at length the happy morning of their reunion came. Her last words were of him, and when they folded her hands on her cold breast, she lay smiling as if she had found death very lovely.

The Gellibrands were a hardy stock, and they throve mightily. They were true loyalists, following the monarch of the time. When the Great Rebellion broke out, they stood for King Charles—with one notable exception. This was Nicholas Gellibrand, youngest son of the Dragon House. He, after long thinking, declared for Parliament.

In wrath and fury, his father drove him forth; erased his name from the records wherein were entered the birth, marriage, and death of them all; and forbade the rest of the family even to name him.

Nicholas fought for his chosen side, with much zeal but little distinction; and it was not until the battle of Worcester that he had a chance to show his mettle. Then he risked his life to extinguish a fire which was creeping perilously near a gunpowder magazine; thereby, no doubt, helping to determine the success of Parliament.

Word was brought to General Cromwell of the deed. He sent for the man, and they looked at each other in silence. Cromwell saw a slight dark-haired fellow, pale of face and weary of eyes, who met his own grim gaze steadily and unflinchingly, and the Lord Protector, as he was to be known, was not ill-pleased.

'I've heard of your doings, young man,' he said curtly. 'Mayhap you have contributed to my crowning mercy. Ask what you will and it shall be yours—save and except the Crown of England,' he added, with a flash of austere humour.

Nicholas Gellibrand looked straightly at him. 'You mean that, sir?'

'Yea!'

'Then grant me that my brother, Stephen Gellibrand, shall not be disturbed in his possession of the Dragon House in the Welsh Marches.'

Cromwell stared at him. 'Why?' he demanded at last.

'Because it hath been ours this hundred and fifty years, and I am loath that it should know a master of another name.'

'Why not ask it for yourself, then?'

'Because I am not the heir. Brother Stephen is that. There be—there *were*—' he corrected himself, 'five brothers between us, who had all a better right than I. I'll not hold what is not mine by right. Stephen hath sons. I'm not wed, nor like to be.'

Cromwell gave way, and Nicholas Gellibrand was sent to the Dragon House with letters binding brother Stephen to keep the peace. So long as he would engage to raise no hand against the Government, the Dragon House was his.

Stephen Gellibrand was a different type of man from his sire. Old Sir Ambrose had died eight years before, and Stephen welcomed his brother with open arms, roared with laughter when he finally dragged out of the young man how Cromwell had been got to leave him his inheritance, and vowed that Nick must bide with them.

Nicholas Gellibrand was very ready to do so. He had had enough of war, and he loved the peace of the Dragon House and its surroundings.

Two years later a very distant cousin of their mother's sent word that her father had died, leaving her a penniless orphan, and she prayed leave to come to her only relatives, the Gellibrands, and serve them, as a poor kinswoman should. Stephen sent his brother to escort the lady thither, and bade him be sure to show her that she was welcome among them.

Nicholas fulfilled his mission faithfully. More, he swiftly realised that unless sweet Loveday Penwarne would agree to be his wife, he could not go on living. She was of the same way of thinking; and when, after many days of the vilest travelling—it was the depth of winter—they reached the Dragon House, it was as plighted lovers. Stephen and his rosy, jolly wife were delighted. The nearest parson was sent for on the spot; and almost before the pair had had time to feel themselves betrothed, they were man and wife.

The Restoration made no difference to any of them. The Dragon House was well off the beaten track in those days, and it is doubtful if his Majesty, King Charles II, ever even heard of the Gellibrands. Nicholas and his wife settled down in a little house built for them at the far west of the estate, and there they lived very happily till Nicholas died at the good old age of eighty-nine, leaving four sons and a faithful widow to mourn him, the twin daughters born to them in the fifteenth year of their marriage having died in their early teens.

For the next two hundred years Gellibrands flourished in the neighbourhood. They thinned their timber. Then they cleared the land and farmed it. The girls were all fresh-faced, sonsy English girls; the boys handsome, brawny fellows. They wedded among the gentry round about, and there seemed no reason why Gellibrands should not be living in the Dragon House until the crack of doom.

But there came a day in 1910 when Sir Ambrose Gellibrand, the then owner of the estate, returning homewards from paying a visit to his newest granddaughter, realised with a shock that, except for himself and his son, the only male Gellibrand left was a distant cousin, descendant of Nicholas the Roundhead, who was farming in New Zealand. He himself had been an only son: his father was killed in a hunting accident a few months after his birth. His uncles had all died unmarried. Of the seven brothers of his grandfather, one had left two daughters who had died childless; one had turned Catholic at the same time as the great Cardinal Newman, and become a monk; one had been killed in a duel, three days before his marriage; and the other four had all died bachelors.

Sir Ambrose was disturbed. Besides his son he had two daughters, one of whom was a militant suffragette, while the other was wholly given over to good works. Neither was likely to wed; but in any case the Dragon House had never gone to any save a Gellibrand by birth.

Two years later a grandson was born, and great were the rejoicings at the Dragon House. He was the last of the grandchildren, and the sturdiest of them. They named him 'Stephen Balthazar,' and thereafter called him 'Peter.'

In 1914 Europe went mad. Sir Ambrose was too old and too full of rheumatism to go to the war; but his son, Balthazar, went with his Hussar regiment, to fall six weeks later at the head of his men. In the days following the receipt of the telegram telling the news, Sir Ambrose became an old man. He, who at fifty-five had been as upright as many a man of thirty-five, was white-haired and bent as if he were twenty years older. And the shot that killed Balthazar Gellibrand killed his widow, who had been ailing at the time. Six months to the day when the news came, her four children were orphans and their grandfather had to be father and mother both.

This roused him from his fury of despair; but not yet was Fate finished with him.

Kate, the suffragette, had sunk her activities in canteen-work.

She caught a chill one bitter night, turned up at her canteen with illness heavy upon her, and died four days later of double pneumonia. Peggy, the charity-worker, married a young naval officer, and a year later died with her newborn son. The terrible pneumonic influenza which, after the war, swept all Europe like a plague, carried off Winifrid, the eldest of the granddaughters. Then Fate held her hand for a time.

The years passed. Peter and his two sisters grew up. He was a handsome, fair-faced fellow, not unlike that young bride the first Balthazar Gellibrand had brought home. His sisters, Gwen and Rosalind, were 'dark' Gellibrands. Then a new blow fell. Gwen, engaged to be married, and preparing happily for her wedding, went through a patch of woodland one spring afternoon to meet her sweetheart. As she passed a certain elm, she realised that though it was a calm day the top was swaying, but it was not till too late that she knew what was happening. The tree was falling, and she tried to escape. But a bough struck her on the temple, and when they found her an hour later, she was dead.

Sir Ambrose mourned his bright-faced granddaughter bitterly, and clung closer yet to the two left him—Peter and Rosalind. Alas for human love! A year later Peter, the idolised heir, was flung from his horse, and injured his spine. For three years he lingered, a helpless invalid, always hopeful and cheery. Then he died, and Rosalind, always the frailest of the four, slipped out of life after him.

It was more than a year later that Sir Ambrose, goaded thereto by his lawyer, agreed that the last heir to the Gellibrand estate must be summoned home to prepare himself for what a short space of years must surely bring him. Sir Ambrose was now a very old man, and he was also a broken one, though the Gellibrand pride and the Gellibrand will, not to mention the Gellibrand temper, forced him to hold his head high and be master still of his wide domains. But death who had robbed him of all his treasures must surely come for him soon. The distant cousin must be recalled to England, and that speedily.

A final blow awaited the old man. Word came from New Zealand, saying that Nicholas Gellibrand, the twelfth holder of the name, had died six months before the urgent letter from the Gellibrand solicitors reached his farm. He left behind him one child, a girl of fourteen, whose mother had died at her birth. At present, this girl was living with her mother's only sister in Invercargill, the Gellibrand farm being in the charge of a capable bailiff, and this aunt refused to yield possession of her niece.

This news roused the old war-horse in Sir Ambrose. Miss Mortimer of Invercargill, N.Z., was given to understand that, unless she yielded up the heiress of the Gellibrands forthwith, the thunders of the law would be invoked. Miss Mortimer's own lawyers were reluctantly forced to inform their client that as her brother-in-law had died intestate, the Gellibrand family had the legal right to claim the child, more especially when a great inheritance like the Dragon House came into the question.

Anne Mortimer was a strong-minded lady, and she would have fought the case through the courts; but her solicitor was too wise to permit it. He pointed out what a bad thing it would be for the child if she were thus dragged into the limelight and Miss Mortimer finally gave way, deep bitterness in her heart. She purchased for her little niece such an outfit as a princess might have owned; loaded her with gifts; and bade farewell to her with dry eyes and an aching heart. As for the child herself, reft from the aunt who had been mother to her since her birth, placed in the charge of a kindly but stranger lady, and shipped off to England whether she would or not, the ensuing chapters will show how she accepted the situation.

Chapter II

THE HEIRESS COMES HOME

IT was a stormy evening in early November when the heiress of the Gellibrands first saw her ancestral home. 'Saw' is, perhaps, scarcely the right word. The rain was pouring down and the wind was skirling wildly through the leafless branches of the trees as the big car swept up the long drive of the Dragon House, bearing within it one slim schoolgirl, whose heart was sinking into her well-cut shoes, and one riotous Alsatian puppy, which had been acquired at some famous kennels only that morning.

Miss Lucas, the lady in whose charge the last of the Gellibrands had travelled, had been greeted at the dock by the news of sickness at her home, which forced her to leave the child after seeing her into the west-bound train at Paddington. It had been with some idea of giving the little girl a sense of companionship that she had broken the journey long enough to take her to the kennels and choose her a puppy.

'If your grandfather, or whatever he is, objects to her too much,' she had said, 'you must find a home for her near by. But I don't suppose he will. Sir Ambrose is well known as a breeder of Alsatians, and a keen dog-fancier.'

'He isn't my grandfather,' returned her charge. 'He's only a very distant cousin—thank goodness!'

Miss Lucas was too much worried to note this remark. They were late, and if their taxi were held up any more, her charge would most likely miss the train. Luckily for the lady, they just managed it, and here, after her long journey, was the last of the Gellibrands arriving at the Dragon House.

The car drew up before the wide stone steps, and on the instant the great door with its heavy iron knocker made in the shape of a dragon flew open, and the child in the car noted a bald-headed, elderly man holding it against the wind. Behind him, in the glow of mellow light that came pouring forth, were what looked to her unaccustomed eyes like an army of trim black-and-white figures, headed by a portly Presence all in black. The chauffeur came round and opened the door of the car, and the girl got out, clutching her puppy to her, and feeling very small and lone as she bravely marched forward up the steps, and in at the big door. It closed behind her, and the Presence rustled forward at once, and greeted her with a friendly smile.

'Miss Gellibrand, I'm shore. Come this way, please, ma'am. The Master is in the liberry, and will see you at once.'

Still hugging the heavy pup, the child followed the rustling gown through the great hall, down a wide corridor, and to a door at the further end. This the Presence opened, saying clearly, 'Miss Gellibrand, sir.' Then she stood aside, and Miss Gellibrand entered, head well up, but fear in her heart, her only consolation that warm, wriggling bundle that she clutched to her.

She came forward into a room of fine proportions. Three of the walls were covered with books. The fourth side was given up to two wide windows, at present closely draped with crimson curtains, and a large painting of a gracious lady in crimson—a Gainsborough, if she had but known it. The furniture was big and massive. Before the log fire which blazed on the hearth stood a wide settee. Opposite it was an armchair in which sat Sir Ambrose. He turned his head and looked at the child as she came up to him, her puppy in her arms, her eyes, full of uncompromising enmity, fixed on his grim face.

He rose to his feet. 'Welcome!' he said shortly.

His young cousin looked at him steadily from under black brows. He noted that she was a 'dark' Gellibrand, with black hair, which she wore in two short, thick plaits, and big dark eyes. Beneath the waveless hair, her brow was square, and so was her jaw. It was not a pretty face, but it was interesting; and she held herself like a princess of the blood.

'Come and sit down,' he said, wheeling up a big chair to the fire. Then his gaze fell on the puppy, and he smiled. 'You have brought your dog?'

'She's only been mine a few hours,' came the reply in a surprisingly deep voice for a child of fourteen. 'Her name is Sanchia.'

'Indeed,' he said courteously. 'And what is yours? I have not heard it, for my solicitor always spoke of you as "Miss Gellibrand," or "Mr Nicholas's daughter."'

The young visitor sat down, disposing Sanchia carefully on her knee. Then she looked at him. 'My name is Jesanne,' she said.

He raised his eyebrows. 'Surely that is a pet name? I never heard it before.'

'It is made up of two names,' explained its owner carefully. 'My mother was Jessica, and my aunt, her sister, is Anne. They put the two names together and made Jesanne of them.'

Sir Ambrose frowned. 'It is not a name of *our* family. Have you no other?'

'Yes—two. I am Jesanne Loveday Balthazar.'

This was a nice quandary. Sir Ambrose had no intention of calling his heiress by any name that would remind him of 'that woman,' as he contemptuously called Miss Mortimer. He would find it difficult to forgive her for her attempt at thwarting him. On the other hand, he detested the name 'Loveday.' 'Balthazar' was obviously out of the question for a girl. If it came to that, in these days it was just as much out of the question for a boy!

Jesanne watched him gravely. There was bitter rebellion in her heart. She had loved her aunt dearly, and had resented being reft from her like this. She had been forced to come to England; but if Sir Ambrose thought he was going to do as he liked with her, he would soon find out his mistake.

'English girls may be ordered about,' she thought, 'but I'll soon show him that New Zealand girls aren't. I'm going to go right on as I've always done.'

Sir Ambrose considered. 'Why the other two?' he asked at length.

'After Father's ancestress and Master Balthazar Gellibrand,' returned Jesanne.

'I cannot think why your father thought he must perpetuate the sentimental name of "Loveday"!' said Sir Ambrose peevishly. 'As for "Balthazar," that's impossible!'

'I know it is.' Jesanne gathered up Sanchia, and stood up. 'I think, Sir Ambrose, we had better understand matters. My name is Jesanne, and I shall never answer to anything else. And I will *never* listen to a word against my father.'

Sir Ambrose looked amazed. Who would have expected this small girl—Jesanne was not only slim, but short for her years—to fly out at him like this?

'I expect you are tired after your journey,' he said stiffly, waiving the question of the name for the moment. He touched a bell. 'Spike shall take you to your rooms, and tea will be sent to you there. Do you wish to take your pup with you, or shall I send her to the kennels with the others?'

'I want her to be with me,' said Jesanne.

There was no time for more, for the door opened, and the Presence—whom Jesanne now recognised as 'Spike'—came in.

'Take Miss Gellibrand to her rooms, Spike,' said her master

curtly. 'See that a tea-tray is taken up to her, and that she has everything she requires.'

'Certainly, sir,' replied Spike. She turned to Jesanne. 'Will you come with me, ma'am?'

Jesanne, still clutching Sanchia to her, turned to follow her from the room. A short word from Sir Ambrose made her stop for a moment.

'We dine at eight. Unless you are very tired, I should be glad of your company.'

'I am not tired, and I will come,' said Jesanne gravely. Then she turned and left him, Spike shutting the door behind her with care.

Up the wide, shallow stairs they went, where the feet of many generations had worn hollows in the treads, and the handrail and banisters were glossy with age and hard polishing. They turned down a corridor, the walls of which were hung with dark portraits. At the end, Spike opened a door and ushered Jesanne into a large room, bright with lamplight and firelight. The walls were hung with a faded, rose-coloured brocade let into panels in the wood, which was black with age. A rose-coloured carpet was on the floor. The furniture was as dark as the woodwork, and on a little dais at one end of the room stood a slender four-post bed, with curtains to match hangings and carpet.

'This is your bedroom, ma'am,' said Spike. 'Your sitting-room is through here.' She opened a door to show another room as gay, but with brocades and carpet of golden-yellow. 'Your bathroom is *here*.'

Jesanne followed her to the other side of the bedroom, where another door opened into a small bathroom, startlingly up-to-date when compared with the rest of the house—or what she had seen of it.

'What a dear little bathroom!' she exclaimed, while Sanchia, whom she had set down, frolicked through to investigate.

'Yes, ma'am. It was a powdering closet, I understand; but Sir Ambrose had it made into a bathroom when he married the late Lady Gellibrand. This is the Dame's Suite, and it was last done up for her ladyship. The bathroom was made modern since we knew you were coming. As you see, ma'am, it is much larger than most powdering closets are, and has a good window. Sir Ambrose's rooms are further down the corridor.'

A tap at the bedroom door interrupted her discourse, and then a pretty, fair-haired country girl came in, clad in the neat black-and-white uniform of the Gellibrand maids.

'That's right, Agnes,' said Spike. 'Miss Gellibrand, this is your own maid, Agnes. She will wait on you, and see to these rooms.'

Jesanne smiled across at the girl. 'Hello, Agnes!' she said. Then she added anxiously, 'I say—mind the pup!' For Agnes was advancing, and Sanchia was ambling playfully before her.

Agnes looked down, and admiration for the pretty creature lit up her face. 'Oh, Miss! What a beauty!' she exclaimed.

The next minute she was called to order. 'Have you brought up the tea-tray for Miss Gellibrand, Agnes?' asked Mrs Spike in awe-inspiring tones.

'No, Mrs Spike,' said Agnes hurriedly. 'But it is all ready.'

'Then please bring it at once. Miss Gellibrand is tired and hungry after her journey, so be quick.'

Agnes vanished, and Mrs Spike turned to Jesanne. 'Let me take your things, ma'am. Have you slippers in that case? And your hairbrush? Shall I turn on the water? You will like to wash your face and hands while Agnes is bringing your tea.'

Jesanne handed over cap, coat, and gloves as composedly as possible, though secretly she felt uncomfortable. She had never been waited on since she could manage her own buttons and strings, and it was rather trying to her sense of independence to be treated so like a baby. She washed her face and hands, and sat with commendable patience while Mrs Spike undid the short plaits which just reached below her shoulders, and brushed out the thick locks.

'Will you wear it loose, ma'am, or shall I plait it again?' inquired the good woman.

'I'll plait it myself, thank you,' said Jesanne, who felt that she had yielded sufficiently, and really must make a stand. She threw a straight look at Mrs Spike as she stood up and began to braid her hair swiftly. 'Agnes is to be my maid, you say. Please, what are you?'

'I am the housekeeper, ma'am.'

'I see. Of course, Sir Ambrose could scarcely be expected to run a place like this himself. Men are such helpless things,' decided Jesanne thoughtfully. Then, as Agnes entered with the tea-tray, she gave a little nod. 'I'll have that in the sitting-room, please, Agnes. Where will you be if I want you?'

Agnes replied that she would come at once if Miss Gellibrand rang the bell. Or she could be unpacking Miss Gellibrand's trunks when they were brought up, which would be in a few minutes.

'I think that *would* be best,' agreed Jesanne. 'All right, Mrs Spike. I shan't need you for the present, thank you.'

'Dismissed me as coolly as if she had had dozens of servants all her life!' declared Mrs Spike later to Mr Totton the butler over a cosy cup of coffee in her own room. 'I'll tell you what it is, Mr Totton; she's a One; that's what she is! And, believe me or believe me not, Sir Ambrose isn't going to find it easy to make *her* do anything she doesn't want to. That's what!'

Chapter III

The First Tussle

At half-past seven, Agnes came to seek her young mistress and bid her change for dinner. She found Jesanne curled up in an armchair, so buried in the book she was reading that the little maid had to speak three times before the young lady heard her.

'If you please, ma'am, it's time to dress for dinner.'

Jesanne lifted her head and surveyed the maid with dreamy eyes. 'What did you say?' she queried.

'It's time to dress for dinner, ma'am. Sir Ambrose is very punctual, and dinner is at eight. There's but 'alf an hour left.'

'I see. Thank you for telling me.' Jesanne felt that whatever else she did, she must not forget her manners in this stately household. She closed her book, laid it aside, and followed Agnes into the bedroom.

Everything was laid out ready for her. Her severely plain frock of black taffeta was on the bed, and Agnes had stitched fresh muslin collar and cuffs into it. Her slippers and silk stockings were waiting, and a dainty muslin petticoat was beside the frock. Jesanne regarded the preparations with secret dismay. At home they had had supper, and as long as she was neat and tidy, Auntie Anne had not worried about much else. If these preparations had to be made each night, it would take up a lot of time. Jesanne was still at the stage when the niceties of the *toilette* are no more than a waste of time. However, she said nothing, but allowed Agnes to help her out of her skirt and jumper, pour out water for washing, brush her hair and tie it loosely back from her face with bows at each side, and put her into the dainty frock. But she made up her mind that a little later on she would speak her mind about this nurse-maiding business. Independent as most Colonials are, she found it hard to submit to being treated like a baby. But it would be too soon to begin that night, so she let it alone, and Agnes found her quite amenable.

Finally, she stood ready, and then, having made sure that the handkerchief Jesanne tucked into the elastic at her knee was immaculate, the little maid led her downstairs to the library door.

'If you'll ring for me when you come up to bed, ma'am, I'll come at once,' she said before she left the girl.

'Thank you, Agnes,' replied Jesanne, 'but I can manage quite well for myself, you know. I'm not a baby!'

'Oh, I know, Miss Jesanne. But young ladies want a bit of maiding at times—young ladies like you, you know.'

Jesanne was about to say that she didn't want 'maiding' at any time, but the friendly look in the honest blue eyes fronting her prevented her from speaking, so all she did was to nod with a smile, and then pass through the door Agnes was holding open, into the library, where Sir Ambrose was sitting awaiting her, spruce in the Englishman's conventional black-and-white of evening wear.

He rose at her entrance, and almost immediately a low, musical rolling sounded. 'Ah, dinner is ready,' he said. 'You are very punctual.'

Jesanne found nothing to reply, so she let him lead her from the library, through the hall, and into a great room, most of which seemed lost in shadows, the only light being a big lamp standing on the table, and casting a rosy glow over the white cloth, the sparkling silver and crystal, and the bowls of yellow chrysanthemums.

Sir Ambrose handed his young cousin to a seat at his right hand;

he himself took the head of the table. Totton the butler waited on them with a dignity and solemnity that froze all Jesanne's conversation.

'How *awful* he is!' she thought as she finished the delicious consommé with which the meal began. 'It's like being waited on by the Sphinx. I wonder if *anything* would make him smile?'

The consommé was followed by crisp whitebait, and an entrée of pheasant. Luckily the portions served were, in Jesanne's case, almost fairylike, for she had eaten a good substantial tea little more than two hours before. The entrée came to an end, and Totton removed the plates and replaced them with a rich trifle, handed to him by his coadjutor, a young footman who looked almost as solemn as he. Sir Ambrose refused the sweet, remarking to his young guest that he was past the age for trifles, but he hoped she would enjoy it. A large plateful was served to her, and she had to struggle through it somehow beneath Totton's suddenly benevolent glance. She felt that to leave any would not only give him an appalling impression of her manners, but grieve him personally.

Trifle was followed by fruit, but Jesanne struck at this. She really could eat no more. Sir Ambrose also declined it, and having finished his burgundy, glanced across at her.

'The honour lies with you,' he said courteously.

Jesanne's mind had been on the vastness of the room, and she had been wondering what it would look like, properly lighted up.

'Not with a stupid lamp, but good old electrics!' she had thought rather contemptuously. Consequently, she did not catch Sir Ambrose's remark,

'Eh?' she said, startled out of politeness. 'I don't understand.'

'I mean that if you have finished, we will go to the library. I have not had the drawing-room opened, as I thought you would prefer to sit with me, or else go to your own sitting-room. Of course, when your governess arrives, we must use it. But it is big, and I prefer the library myself.'

But Jesanne was paying no heed to the latter part of his speech. The first part was employing all her mind. A *governess*! This must be seen to at once! She felt that she had no use for a governess. In New Zealand she had attended one of the excellent girls' schools there, and it wasn't likely she was going to agree to anything so old-fashioned and boring as a private governess. However, the question was destined not to be thrashed out that night.

Once they were seated in the library, and after Sir Ambrose had asked and received permission to smoke—he treated his small cousin with the same stately courtesy he would have shown a lady five times her age—he made a statement which brought the pair of them to the edge of war.

'I hope you find your rooms comfortable?' he began.

'Quite, thank you,' replied Jesanne.

'I think you will find Agnes Hiles a good maid,' he went on, giving her no chance to tell him that she did not want a maid of *any* kind. 'If you do not, you must tell Spike, and she will discharge her and find you another.'

'I like what I have seen of her, thank you,' said Jesanne, 'but, Sir Ambrose—'

But he was already asking her if her puppy seemed likely to settle down happily, and she had to reply that Sanchia seemed quite happy, so far.

'You must expect her to cry for her mother and the rest of the litter at first,' he told her. 'All pups do—especially at night. Has she had anything to eat? Yes? Then she ought to sleep all night and you will have no trouble with her. But she is bound to fret a little at first.'

Jesanne knew this. In New Zealand she had always had a dog, and she remembered how Mollie, the beloved cocker she had left behind with Auntie Anne, had made night hideous with her yells for the first two or three nights after she had left her mother.

However, this was not settling the governess question. She sat upright, both mentally and physically, for she felt instinctively that Sir Ambrose, having once made his plans, would be hard to move.

'Sir Ambrose,' she began.

He lifted his eyes from the burning logs which he had been studying and said, 'Yes—what is it? And, by the way, as we are kin, and as this is your home, don't you think it would be better if you called me "Cousin Ambrose"?'

'Oh, I couldn't do that!' exclaimed Jesanne. 'It would seem so—so familiar!'

'Not when you do it by my wish,' he assured her.

Jesanne could scarcely tell him to his face that he seemed far too old to her to be addressed in any save the most formal manner, so she only went pink and murmured, 'I'll try, then.'

'Thank you. And I have been thinking it over, and I have decided to call you "Jessie" if you have no objection.'

He added the last phrase from sheer courteous habit, for it never dawned on him that the child could really object to such a simple solving of the difficulties of her name. But he soon found his mistake. Jesanne bristled up like a little turkey-cock.

'I have every objection,' she told him. 'I loathe the name—always have. And anyway, it *isn't* my name—my name is Jesanne, and I never answer to anything else.'

'Unfortunately,' he said suavely, 'I dislike the name. I dislike all compounds of the kind, and prefer not to use them. The name "Loveday" I dislike as much; and, as I said before, "Balthazar" is out of the question.'

An obstinate look came over Jesanne's face. She squared her jaw, and said, 'My name is Jesanne. My father and mother chose it for me, and I have always been called by it. I won't answer to anything else!'

'Don't be a foolish child,' he said, throwing the end of his cigar into the fire. 'Of course you will do as you are told.'

'I will not answer to Jessie!' was the swift reply. Then, in a tone of scorn, '*Jessie! Jessie Gellibrand!* It sounds like an advertisement for face-cream, or cocoa, or something! No, Sir Ambrose! My name is Jesanne, and I'm going to stick to it!'

A frown came between Sir Ambrose's brows. He was determined not to yield. He wished to remove from the child all associations with her early life. She was to become a true daughter of the Dragon House, and forget, as far as possible, her Colonial beginnings. Not her father, of course; but then, he had been a Gellibrand. But she could have no recollections of her mother; and the sooner she forgot this aunt of hers, the better. The Dragon House would brook no divided allegiance. The child must be Gellibrand in thought, and deed, and word. If part of her heart were with Miss Anne Mortimer across the seas, how could that be?

'I am sorry you should regard it in that way,' he said, keeping his temper by a determined effort. 'However, as you have such a prejudice against the name, let us make it "Jess." That is short, and not too common. We will not quarrel over a matter of two letters, you and I. We will make it "Jess."' And he looked at her with a smile, well pleased at having, as he thought, really found a way out of the difficulty.

'Oh no, we won't!' cried Jesanne, springing to her feet. 'I'll be Jesanne or nothing! Call me "Jess" or "Jessie" if you like, but don't expect me to answer to it, for I won't. I'll answer to nothing but my proper name. I might have agreed to "Loveday," though I think it's a soppy name. But I'll *never* agree to any shortening of "Jesanne." I— I'm proud of it! It's not like anyone else!'

Sir Ambrose had risen when she jumped up. He was annoyed,

but not even his annoyance could make him forget what was due to any female, even when she was as young as Jesanne. In a dim sort of way, the child recognised that such courtesy was unusual, and rather liked it, under the hot flame of anger that had risen in her. Colonial as she was, she had enough of the Gellibrand blood in her to appreciate the unwonted charm of such manners.

Now he looked down at her, and for a moment his eyes gleamed with amusement as he realised what a very small person it was who had thus bidden him defiance. But the amusement faded. Sir Ambrose was a martinet by both nature and training. Such behaviour to himself was not to be tolerated in a chit of fourteen. However, the child was, doubtless, tired. He would make allowances.

'I think you are tired,' he said quietly. 'Perhaps you would like to go to bed? I will send for your maid, and we will resume this conversation tomorrow after you have rested.'

He touched the bell, and when Totton appeared, asked him to send Miss Gellibrand's maid to her young mistress's rooms at once. When the old man had departed, he turned to his inwardly fuming guest.

'I will bid you good-night, my dear. Agnes will be waiting for you upstairs, and I am sure you are in need of rest. Breakfast is at nine in the morning; but if you are tired, please don't trouble to come down. We must not forget what a very long journey you have had. Good night to you.'

He held out his hand, and there was nothing for it but to take it—which Jesanne did, very reluctantly. Then he crossed the room and held the door open for her. Jesanne could only go out with head held high. Inwardly, she was furious. However politely he might put it, this dismissal was simply sending her to bed as if she were a naughty baby of three. Fourteen was not going to take that sort of thing sitting down; and Sir Ambrose would have been better advised if he had contrived to exercise a little more patience. Patience, however, was never a commodity which the Gellibrands possessed in large stocks. One reason why the war between the old man and the small girl was likely to be long and stubborn was that both were too much alike—true Gellibrands. Neither was likely to give way easily; and neither, it was certain, would ever yield without a struggle.

In this instance, Jesanne, as she mounted the old staircase, was forced to admit that so far Sir Ambrose had scored all along the line. She knew she had answered him rudely, and he had never, for one moment, been moved from his old-world courtesy. But though she secretly admired him for this, she set her teeth and vowed that she would not be coerced. She would show him!

With this unpraiseworthy sentiment she entered her room, to find Agnes waiting for her, and Sanchia raising an adorable little pointed face from her hamper as her mistress entered.

Chapter IV

A Truce is Made

JESANNE was tired, as Sir Ambrose had shrewdly suspected. Once she was safely in bed, she fell asleep, and she slept on till long past her usual hour for waking. She never heard Agnes come in at six to pick up Sanchia, who had behaved like a little lady all night, and carry her off for an early-morning run. Carver, the kennelman at the Dragon House, had, on hearing that Miss Gellibrand had brought a dog with her, bidden the young maid let him have it early in the morning for the sake of its manners. So Sanchia was taken down to the kennels, where she found assorted babies of various ages, and had a glorious time among them all.

At half-past seven the baby was fed with the others, and then Agnes came to retrieve her, and bore her back to the schoolroom, where a bright fire was crackling in the grate and the pale November sunshine lit up the room. The maid put the pup into her hamper, and then peeped in at her young mistress. Jesanne was still asleep, and Sir Ambrose had given orders the night before that she was to be left to sleep as long as she would, and her breakfast taken up to her when she roused. The maid left her, therefore, and went to seek her own meal.

It was nine o'clock before Jesanne stirred. Then, hearing a little whimpering noise, she sat up, rubbing her eyes to clear them of the sleep-mists.

'Where in the world—oh, the Dragon House, of course!' she exclaimed aloud. She glanced out of the window. 'I wonder what the time is?'

She burrowed under the pillow for her watch, and examined it with horror in her eyes. 'Five past nine! How awful!' Then she stretched and yawned. 'Oh, well! I don't suppose it really matters. Sir Ambrose did say last night that I was to stay in bed if I was tired. I must have been, to sleep like that!'

A louder whimper reminded her of the pup, and she tumbled out on to the floor. 'That's Sanchia! I hope they've attended to her before this!'

She found her dressing-gown and bedroom slippers, and then ran in next door, where she found Agnes laying a dainty breakfast-table.

'Good morning, Agnes,' she said pleasantly.

'Good morning, Miss Gellibrand,' returned Agnes. 'Will you get up now, ma'am? Breakfast will be ready by the time you are dressed.'

'What about Sanchia?' demanded Jesanne.

'She's been down to kennels, miss, and Carver has fed her. She's had a good run with the other pups. I think she'll do until you go out for your walk with Sir Ambrose.'

'Oh?' This was news to Jesanne. However, Agnes was already moving to the bathroom to turn on her bath, so she dropped a kiss on the head of the pup and then went off. Half an hour later, she was seated at the table, eating breakfast with gusto, and asking sundry questions of Agnes.

When the meal was ended, the maid brought her hat and coat and gloves, for Sir Ambrose had sent up a message to the schoolroom that he was going out at ten, and, if Jesanne was ready, he would be glad if she would accompany him.

'I suppose I'd better,' was Jesanne's comment on hearing this.

But though she got into hat and coat, she baulked at the gloves. 'Gloves—for the garden? Good heavens, no!'

'I expect you'll be going down to the village, ma'am,' said Agnes.

'Well, even so, I don't need gloves. Take them away, Agnes. It's not cold enough for gloves yet.'

Agnes put them away, though she guessed that Sir Ambrose would look askance at a young lady without gloves. But there was no gainsaying Miss Gellibrand. Her tone was commanding.

Jesanne called Sanchia, and went out of the room and along the corridor. She had refused her maid's offer of escort. She felt that she must begin to find her own way about the big house as soon as possible. This was easy enough, for the head of the stairs lay at the far end of the corridor, and on looking down, she saw the great hall she had seen the night before, with its suits of armour and clusters of weapons, and great carved hearth. Standing by one of the heavily mullioned windows was the tall, somewhat awe-inspiring figure of Sir Ambrose, a magnificent specimen of the English mastiff standing beside him. At sight of the dog, Jesanne picked up Sanchia, who was all for bundling down the stairs, and went slowly down, a dignified little figure in her big black hat and grey coat.

Sir Ambrose heard the light patter of her footsteps, and looked up as she reached the foot of the stairs. Without greeting her in any way, he took a stride forward. 'Wait!' he said imperiously.

Jesanne stood still, wondering why. He came up to her, and laid a hand on her arm. 'A friend, Beowulf! A mistress for you!'

The child saw the huge dog coming behind his master, and guessed at once why her cousin had been so peremptory. Shifting Sanchia to one arm, she held out the other hand to Beowulf, who sniffed it, then licked it, and finally turned an inquiring gaze on the bright-eyed puppy who was stretching her neck to sniff at him.

'You may let the pup run,' said Sir Ambrose. 'Beowulf is a gentleman, and never interferes with anything smaller than himself. But he is getting old, and is inclined to be suspicious of fresh human beings. However, he is your friend and guard now.'

Jesanne set down Sanchia, who promptly ran up to the big dog and wagged an ingratiating tail. Beowulf bent his head to sniff at her; then he raised it again, and coming to the little girl, laid it against her. Jesanne promptly put her hand on his magnificent head, and looked into the sunken eyes.

'Friends, Beowulf?' she asked.

Beowulf wagged his tail.

Sir Ambrose had been watching them, and he nodded approvingly to himself as he noticed the child's fearlessness. She was a true Gellibrand there. Every Gellibrand loved his dogs, and for generations back, every Gellibrand had bred them.

'Beowulf recognises a real friend,' he said, his rather cold voice softening a little. 'Now we will call Donna and Storm, and go for a stroll.'

Donna and Storm proved to be Alsatians, litter brother and sister, and a handsome pair with their black-and-gold coats, prick ears, and beautiful heads. They were quite young, and ready to adopt Sanchia as a playfellow. At Sir Ambrose's suggestion, Jesanne let the pup run with them, though she was not able to keep up with them when they pranced ahead, wild with joy. Old Beowulf paced sedately beside his master, and so the party began to make the rounds.

They first walked the terrace which encircled three sides of the house—looking eastwards to the Malvern Hills; north to the Black Mountains; west and south to Gloucestershire and the Cotswolds.

'What glorious views!' said Jesanne, as they came back to the front of the house and began to go down the long avenue.

'This is one of England's loveliest counties,' replied Sir Ambrose. 'Turn off here, child. I will take you up to Balthazar's Mound, and then you can see our boundaries.'

They turned along a side-path which led upwards to the summit of a well-wooded mound which Jesanne had already noticed. At first they went through tall pines and larches, so thickly planted that the path was narrow. But as they neared the summit the trees thinned out, until they finally reached the top, and she found herself on a tiny grassy plateau, with only a few gorse-bushes here and there and an ancient thorn-tree.

Sir Ambrose pointed his stick at the thorn-tree. 'That is said to have grown from a slip of the famous Glastonbury thorn. It was planted by the first Balthazar Gellibrand's bride during the first year of their marriage, and is, therefore, more than four hundred years old. Now look. Do you see that silver thread in the distance?' His stick pointed far away. 'That is the Ddwyvyll, which flows round three sides of the estate, and joins one of the lesser tributaries of the Wye. Formerly we held land beyond it; but we have been obliged to sell part at various periods. But never more than we can avoid. We Gellibrands love the land.'

'I think—I can—understand that—a little,' said Jesanne slowly.

He turned and looked at her. 'I am glad to hear that. It is one of the marks of the true Gellibrand. Now, come. We will walk through the park to the east gate. Then I can show you the village. We must make the most of this week,' he added, 'for after that your governess will be here, and you will be busy in the mornings.'

Jesanne remained silent. She meant to let him know that she did not approve of the governess idea; but she wanted to hold her tongue for the present if she could. She possessed another Gellibrand characteristic, of which, at present, he knew nothing—a flaming temper. She felt that there would be a battle royal over her education, and she was not sure of her own powers of self-control. She could scarcely indulge in a rage when she had just arrived, so she was resolved to say as little as possible for the present.

It was a glorious day. The sky was blue and serene, with white cloud-galleons floating across it. A fresh breeze blew through the pines, stinging Jesanne's dark cheeks to a warm glow. The trees were nearly leafless, but here and there a copper beech still retained much of its autumn beauty and stood glowing in the sunshine. As she looked round with eager, beauty-loving eyes, Jesanne thought to herself that Master Gellibrand had chosen well when he had chosen this fair valley for his home.

'I wonder what made him do it?' she said aloud.

Sir Ambrose jumped, for he had been buried in his sad thoughts of the boy who should have inherited the Gellibrand estates, but had met death first. 'Who?' he asked.

'Balthazar Gellibrand,' said Jesanne. 'He came from Kent, didn't he?'

The old man turned a more kindly look on her than he had yet given her. 'Yes. Who taught you that—your father?'

Jesanne shook her head. 'Daddy never had time for anything of that kind. Farming is a whole-time job in New Zealand. And at nights he was too tired to want to do anything but play. It was my aunt. Daddy had a book with some of the history of the Gellibrands written down in it, and she used to read it to me every Sunday afternoon.'

Despite himself, Sir Ambrose felt rising in him a kindlier feeling for the lady he had hitherto regarded with unmitigated dislike. But all he said was, 'Indeed? And what history did it give you?'

'Not very much,' said Jesanne. 'It told the story of Master Balthazar's coming to the valley, and how he built the Dragon House, and about Mistress Cecily Hussey, whom he married and brought here. But there was not much else. It was written by my grandfather, and he only began it a few weeks before he was drowned when he was yachting off the coast, and he had done very little. They never found his body,' she added.

'I remember hearing of it,' said Sir Ambrose. 'He was a young man; he would have been twenty years younger than I had he lived. I have outlived all my relations, child— except you.'

Jesanne coloured. She still could not feel that he was her kinsman, and many of his views seemed absurd to her, brought up in the democratic atmosphere of New Zealand. Why, for instance, should the great estate be considered before her happiness? And yet, already she was beginning to feel more kindly towards it. But he was going on with his speech, and she must attend.

'I want you to know all the tenants, child. Most of them have had their farms handed down from father to son for generations, and are as much part of the valley as we are. They belong to the family, as, years ago, tenants and servants always did belong to the family they served. The head of the Dragon House has always felt responsibility for his people, and I wish you to learn to feel that responsibility. When I am gone—and it cannot be many years now; I am an old man and have lived my four-score years and more—I should like to feel that you will take up the burden I shall lay down. Remember, our motto is "Service." Gellibrands have always served their dependants. I want you to keep up the tradition.'

Jesanne looked serious. 'It sounds like—like Queen Victoria when they told her she would be queen,' she murmured.

'And you know what her answer was?' He stopped and looked at the child.

Jesanne nodded. 'Oh yes; I know. But I think—I think it's all rather frightening.'

His eyes softened as he looked at the little figure. 'No; for it will come gradually. Listen to me, child. I am willing to be friends if you will. I have been thinking the matter over. Your name was chosen by your father. I will accept that. I will call you "Jesanne" as you wish. In return, I ask you to accept your governess without comment. At least make a trial of her. You may like her. I am told that she is a very clever woman, and an excellent teacher. For the sake of peace, will you give her a fair trial?'

Jesanne thought hard. 'I will,' she said at length, stretching out to him a slim, chilly paw. 'I would much rather go to school; but I will see what having a governess is like. Sir Ambrose, if it is not a success, will you let me try my way?'

It was his turn to think. 'It will be difficult,' he said slowly. 'There is no day-school near enough for you. If you go to boarding-school, it means that you will be away from the Dragon House the greater part of the year. I will promise you this. If she is not a success, I will dismiss her, and get someone else. Will that do?'

Jesanne was very unwilling to agree. But he had given way a good deal, and she could do no less. 'Very well,' she said reluctantly. 'Then that is agreed. And now, Sir Ambrose, *may* I have a race with the dogs?'

'Yes; run along,' he said. 'Mind they don't knock you over. Donna and Storm are apt to be rough.'

Jesanne laughed, and went ahead. She ran fleetly and well, head up, elbows in, like a boy. The dogs raced after her, even Baby Sanchia, who, however, soon gave it up. She had had a good romp already and they had had a long walk. She waited till Sir Ambrose came up to her, and then rolled over on her back, her four legs in the air, begging to be picked up and carried. He smiled, gathered the leggy little thing into his arms, and stood waiting till Jesanne, her cheeks crimson, her eyes bright, came flying back, followed by Donna and Storm, who were leaping madly round her, and barking joyously.

'Now we must go home to lunch,' he said, as the child stood panting beside him. 'I hope you aren't too tired. We have still a mile to go.'

Jesanne laughed breathlessly. 'I'm not tired. What a huge place to belong to one man!'

'Surely no bigger than your farms in New Zealand?' he said, as he set Sanchia down to run beside them, and called the other dogs sharply to heel.

'No; but they are used for sheep, and work, you know. You don't do any work here.'

'That wood,' he said, pointing back to the pinewood on the mound, 'is used for any building that goes on here. So is the one right over there; it is beech, elm, and oak. We never buy a plank of timber here. And we never cut down a tree unless it is necessary. And whatever tree is cut down, is always replaced by a sapling of the same kind. That is another of our traditions. The result is that our woods never grow less. Even in the last war, when so much had to be cut for the Government, we replanted as fast as we cut down. I have a forestry man in charge, and we pride ourselves on our beautiful timber.'

'What heaps of traditions there are!' said Jesanne. 'It seems a tremendous lot to learn.'

'As I have told you, it will come by degrees. Don't be afraid, Jesanne. You will learn it all in time. And perhaps,' he added, 'knowing that there is so much will reconcile you to having lessons at home. You will try, won't you?'

'I'll try. But you don't know how much I shall miss all the fun of school!' she added.

'You shall have other fun,' he promised her. 'Now come along, or we shall be late. I'll take you for a drive this afternoon.'

Chapter V

The House Itself

Man proposes and God disposes. They did not get their drive that afternoon. The sky was clouding over as they entered the great door, and as they sat down to luncheon the rain came with all the lash and fury of a November storm.

'Too wet, even for the car,' said Sir Ambrose. 'What shall we do instead? What would you like, Jesanne?'

'Please,' said Jesanne, 'I'd like, more than anything else, to go all over the house.'

'Very well,' he said. 'Take an hour to read or anything else you like, and be ready for me at half-past two. Mind you put on a wrap. If you're to see everything—as far as we know everything nowadays—we must go into rooms that are rarely opened, and that will be very cold. Finished? Then run along to the schoolroom, and come to me in the library at half-past two, as I said.'

Jesanne went off, followed by Sanchia, Donna, and Storm, while old Beowulf went with his master. The three Alsatians settled down comfortably on the hearth-rug, and the young mistress curled herself up beside them, and gave way to wild speculations as to what her cousin had meant by saying, 'as far as we know everything nowadays.' Could there be a secret room? Perhaps there was hidden treasure! The Dragon House was just the place for that sort of thing, decided Jesanne joyfully. Oh, how thrilling if she should find something! The leaping imagination of fourteen sprang higher than usual at the bare idea, and she was nearly late in the library. Nearly; but not quite. The chiming of the pretty clock on the mantelpiece reminded her of her appointment, and snatching up the loose cloak she had brought from her bedroom in readiness, she flung it over her shoulders and tore off downstairs, accompanied by the entire pack.

Sir Ambrose shook his head when he saw them. 'No; we'll take Beowulf, but not these wild animals. Ring the bell, Jesanne, please, and Totton shall send for Carver to take them to kennels. They can romp in the covered yard.'

Jesanne rang the bell, while her cousin pulled on his overcoat, and when Totton arrived, he was asked to send for the kennel-man, and have the other dogs removed to kennels. Then Sir Ambrose picked up two electric torches lying on the table, handed one to his small cousin, and led the way up the stairs.

Up and up they went. The Dragon House was four good storeys high, with cellars below the ground floor, as Jesanne was to find out. Master Balthazar had erected a small Manor; but his descendants had added to it from time to time; and now it sprawled, long, high, rambling, over a great space. It possessed the original front, with wings which stretched out back and front, so that the shape was that of a wide capital H, thus:

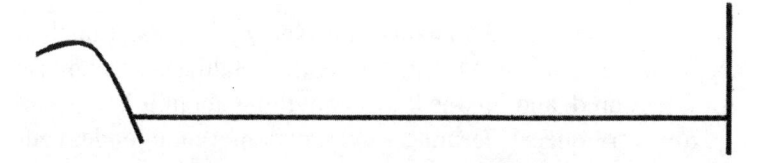

The front wings embraced the lawns with their formal beds and borders. The back ones formed the walls for the great stable-yard. In the main portion of the house, the rooms all faced on to the lawns, the windows at the back lighting the hall, which was open to the roof. Long corridors ran behind the rooms, linking up the main part with the wings, the staircases being in those parts, after the great main stairs had reached the first gallery. Jesanne knew this, for her own rooms were in the south wing. She had wondered why the stairs should have ended so abruptly. Now she put the question.

'Cousin Ambrose, how did they get upstairs before the other wings were built on? Or was the house only two storeys high at first?'

Sir Ambrose looked at her a little strangely. 'You are quick, child. That is one of the mysteries of the family. It is known from the old records that Balthazar Gellibrand built his house three storeys high. The attics were added about seventy years after his death. The north wing was built by Caspar Gellibrand, son of Sir Stephen, and nephew of your own ancestor, Nicholas, in the reign of James II. The south wing was the work of Ambrose Gellibrand, guardian of young Sir Stephen, under the second George. The old staircase had disappeared by that time but we have no record of its destruction, and, indeed, Ambrose writes that though he knows it existed before the Civil War, no trace of it had ever been found in his day, and its disappearance was a mystery.'

'But a staircase can't *disappear*!' exclaimed Jesanne. 'It's such a *big* thing!'

Sir Ambrose nodded. 'That is true. And yet it is also true that, except for the stairs we have just ascended, Balthazar's staircase *has* disappeared, and no one knows anything about it.'

'How very queer!' Jesanne's eyebrows met in an endeavour to solve the mystery. 'What do *you* think can have happened, Cousin Ambrose?'

'I was inclined to think it had been bricked up at the time of the building of the south wing. But I have had experts here, and they all say that there is no sign of it. Neither is there any sign of its having been taken down. This,' he tapped it as he spoke, 'is the original panelling put up by Balthazar's orders, and it shows no marks anywhere of having been, at any time, built over.'

Jesanne stared up at the panelling, black with age, and brought to a high state of glossiness by the hard rubbing of generations. It showed an elaborate design of angels. Singing angels, angels playing on strange instruments, such as she had never seen before, angels with heads bent in perpetual adoration, angels drifting across the panels on sleeping wings—all these thronged and crowded the black wood.

'Balthazar had all these carved in Germany, always famous—in the south, at any rate—for its wood-carvers,' said Sir Ambrose. 'How he got them here, Heaven knows! But he did, and here they have been, ever since. This is known as the Angel Gallery. Look up! Those heads that form a frieze are angels' heads.'

'It's—wonderful!' gasped Jesanne. 'However did they do it?'

'The South Germans, of that day at least, were a race of artists. But you can see for yourself that there is no sign of any staircase here. And Balthazar was a practical man, who would never have hidden his carvings under a staircase.'

'Perhaps they ran where the entrance to the wing is,' suggested Jesanne.

'No; for the opening is too narrow, and it would have been too steep. Besides, in that case, there must have been some mention of it in the records, and there is none.'

'Could it have been built into the wall, perhaps?'

Sir Ambrose shook his head. 'The panels cover the walls. Besides, thick as they are, I doubt if they are thick enough to have taken even a spiral.'

'Then it *is* a mystery. How thrilling!'

Sir Ambrose smiled. 'You must try to solve it for us. I would give a good deal to know just what has happened. Shall we go up? I thought we had better start with the attics and come down. The days are short now.'

Jesanne obediently followed him along the corridor to the south wing and up the handsome stairway to the next storey. Here, the old part of the house, that is, the walls of the gallery, were adorned with hunting scenes, almost as wonderful as the angels of the one below.

'The Hunters' Gallery,' said Sir Ambrose. 'There is no carving on the one above. It was added at a much later date, and the builder was contented with plain panelling. All this woodwork is one reason why I have set my face against having the house wired for electricity. There have been too many bad accidents since electric light came in for me to venture to risk it.'

Jesanne, who, on her first evening, had thought contemptuously of the lamps and candles, was silent. She could see the point. 'Isn't it awfully valuable?' she asked.

He shrugged his shoulders. 'They tell me it is. I have been asked more than once to sell even one panel to wealthy Americans. Museums have made me offers for some of it. But we don't sell part of our house, Jesanne. Remember that!'

Jesanne nodded. 'It would be like—like—like selling its soul, almost,' she said thoughtfully.

'Exactly. I am glad you recognise the fact.'

By this time they had reached the top storey, and Jesanne was looking at the plain panelling of the last gallery. But if it was disappointing after the beauties of the other two, the high railings that ran round the outer side were beautiful with their graceful curves and perfect proportions.

'Every year,' said her cousin, 'an expert comes to examine all the woodwork. It is so old that I have it watched carefully. In my grandfather's time, we got the deathwatch beetle in the floor of this gallery. It was discovered quite accidentally by a maid who was polishing the boards, and felt one give under her rubbing. She had the sense to tell the housekeeper, who reported it at once, and it was found that the greater part of the front and this side was rotten. It was all refloored; and since then, careful watch has been kept on all of it.'

'What wood is this?' asked Jesanne, touching the woodwork.

'Satinwood. The Angel Gallery and the Hunters' Gallery are of Spanish walnut. Do you know why?'

Jesanne shook her head. 'I've no idea. Because it is dark, or something?'

'No; because it is the one wood that never gets worm in it. You will find it used in many old churches for that reason. We have never watched the panelling there because of that, but in case of other troubles. Now, come and see the rooms.'

He led her from room to room. Many of them were just servants' bedrooms, all comfortable, and gay, but very commonplace. Two or three were used as boxrooms and storerooms, and Jesanne would have loved to linger to examine the various treasures stored there. But already the light was fading, and her cousin hurried her on.

'Here is something that will interest you,' he said at length, turning the key in one door with some difficulty. He got it open, and ushered her into a long, narrow room, with raised dais at one end. A faint, greenish light filtered through the lancet-shaped window above the dais. In the wall, near the door, was what the child described to herself as 'a kind of hollow.' She got the impression that she was not in an ordinary room, though, so far as she could see, it was empty. Sir Ambrose switched on his powerful torch, holding it above his head, and sending the light flashing all round.

'Well? Do you know what it is?' he asked.

Jesanne shook her head. 'No,' she said in hushed tones.

'It is the old chapel,' he told her. 'Gellibrands remained Catholics up to the days of William and Mary—that is, through the worst of the penal times. This was the chapel. You know, don't you, that a chapel must never have another room over it—only the roof? When the bad days for Catholics came, and men had to worship in secret, or pay for their worship with their lives, this was made. At that time, the door was hidden behind panelling, and was only to be opened by a spring. See here!'

Still holding the torch, he went forward, and bent to fumble with something at one side of the wall. There was a groaning and a rumbling, and then, before Jesanne's fascinated eyes, two great doors slid out of the walls, coming together and completely hiding the dais.

'Was the altar there?' she asked.

'Yes; and you can understand that this was a convenient way to hide it. Bales of goods, and oddments, were kept here, and if any men found the door and opened it, they saw only a windowless corner which was used for storing things.' He touched the spring again, and the doors slid back. 'Come up here, Jesanne. Do you see this niche? That is an aumbry—where the stocks of sacred wine and oils were kept. Now stoop down and feel round that stone. There's a roughness there. Got it? Then press—hard.'

Jesanne pressed with all her force, and, to her amazement, a whole block of the wall, perhaps four feet by two, swung back, disclosing under the light of the torch a narrow stone staircase.

'Is it—is it a priest's hole?' she gasped excitedly.

'Yes. If the hounds were on the scent, the priest could secure his sacred vessels, slip through here, and go down there. Come along, and I'll show you.'

Jesanne went with him at once. The steps were terribly steep and narrow, and she thought to herself that the priests must have been thin men to slip up and down easily. The staircase wound down and down for some considerable way. Then it stopped before a heavily barred door. Sir Ambrose selected a great key from the bunch in his hand, and giving her the torch to hold, inserted it in the lock, and slowly turned it. Then he beckoned her to follow him, and she went in, and found herself in a slip of a room, furnished with only a wooden stool, a small table, and a crucifix on the wall. It was lighted by two holes which were, as she could see when the torch had been put out, almost overgrown with ivy. She looked round with awe.

'How dreadful to be here, with men hunting for you just above, and know that if they caught you they would hang you!' she said with a shiver. 'Was there no way of escaping?'

'Naturally—just as there was a secret way of entering. Slip your finger into that knot-hole over there. It will lift quite easily.'

Jesanne stooped down, slipped a finger into the knot-hole, and heaved. At once one of the wide boards came up, disclosing more stairs, down which she peered excitedly. A blast of cold, dank air came up, to blow the hair from her face and send the folds of her cloak swirling. She looked round interrogatively at Sir Ambrose.

'If it were a good day,' he said, bringing the torch close and sending the light down into the depths that she might see, 'I would take you down, but I'm afraid the passage will be full of pools. It leads right under the house, as far as Balthazar's Mound, where there is a fork. If the priest thought it well, he could turn up and come out on the Mound. That entrance has now fallen in, however. But the other, which takes one five miles hence, is still in existence, though no one knows of it but myself and Mr Jennings, my agent. You, as the heir, must know of it, of course. I will show you some day. It comes out in a little gully among rocks, and from there, the priests could get up into the heart of the mountains.'

'Were any of them ever captured?' asked Jesanne.

'Yes,' he said shortly.

She heaved a deep sigh. 'I'm glad I live in a time where you can be what you like without other people interfering. It must have been ghastly!'

Sir Ambrose nodded, and stooped down and replaced the board. 'Come along! You've been here long enough. I don't want you to celebrate coming to England by catching a cold.'

They went back up the narrow, twisting stairs, and into the old chapel. Jesanne looked at it, while her cousin made all secure.

'It looks so deserted. Why don't you fit it up again, Cousin Ambrose? You could have prayers here, couldn't you?'

'I could; but I'm not going to,' said Sir Ambrose, ushering her out of the place, and leading her back along the corridor to the staircase. 'For one thing, it has always been a Catholic chapel, and though we Gellibrands are Catholics no longer, we have always had a feeling against turning it into a place for Protestant worship. For another, it is too far out of the way. Poor old Totton, and even Spike, would find it rather a task to struggle up here twice a day. Finally, it is, as I say, a Gellibrand secret.'

'I thought that meant only the priest's hole,' said Jesanne.

'No; it means everything. In the early days, it was necessary to keep it a secret from all except those who could be trusted. Later, I suppose it had become a tradition. Don't talk about it, child, will you? We Gellibrands are very tenacious of our traditions.'

Jesanne nodded. 'I see. No; I won't talk about it. Where now?'

'We'll do the south wing on the Hunters' Gallery. Not that there's much to see. But you'll like the room where, so it is said, Caspar Gellibrand, who was out with Prince Charlie in the Forty-five, lay hidden for eight weeks, disguised as his father's old cousin Anna, and supposed to be suffering from smallpox.'

'But—how could he? Didn't anyone know?' asked Jesanne.

'The poor old lady had died the night he fled to his home,' explained Sir Ambrose. 'Luckily, only Lady Gellibrand was with her at the time. She roused Sir Michael—he was the father of young Sir Stephen—and between them they managed to get Mistress Anna into the priest's hole, and substitute Caspar for her. Sir Michael had always been fond of Caspar, who was his youngest brother, and later, he found means of getting the boy away to France, where he died six years later.'

'How sweet of Lady Gellibrand!' said Jesanne.

'She seems to have been a very delightful woman. Stephen was only a baby when it all happened, and Sir Michael died three years later—broke his back out hunting. As you'll find out, Jesanne, about one out of every three Gellibrands die in their beds. The rest of us finish otherwise.'

'How did Stephen die?' asked Jesanne.

'Fell from the top gallery where he was walking round the parapet for a wager. He was a wild spark. He left three sons, two of whom fell in battle. The third, Sir Ambrose, died at the respectable age of ninety of a fit of apoplexy. He was one of the reputable Gellibrands.'

He opened a door as he spoke, and drew her into a big, rather gloomy bedroom, with hangings of sage-green, faded and worn. Heavy mahogany furniture filled the room, and the big four-post bed was covered with a wonderful embroidered counterpane.

'This is as Caspar left it,' explained Sir Ambrose. 'They had a grand funeral, with a coffin filled with earth and stones, after he had gone. Poor old Anna was smuggled into the family vault during the eight weeks, by the way. Sir Michael had a body-servant who was dumb, and his foster-brother into the bargain. The very mention of smallpox was enough to keep most folk away from the room—including the Hanoverian troops. But it was a daring thing to do.'

'But it panned out all right. I think it was thrilling,' said Jesanne.

'Thrilling, all right. But there goes the gong, and that means that tea is ready. We must leave the rest of the place for another day. Come along now, and have your tea.'

Jesanne laughed. 'I must wash, first. Some of those places weren't exactly—clean.' She spread out a pair of very grubby hands as she spoke.

'Run along, then. Tea is in the library, I suppose, as usual. Be quick. I dislike cold tea.'

Jesanne scampered off, and Sir Ambrose, with old Beowulf, who had followed them everywhere, pressed close to his side, looked after her.

'I believe,' he said thoughtfully to the great dog, 'I believe I shall become fond of her. She seems a nice child in some ways. That woman hasn't done so badly for the Dragon House after all.'

Chapter VI

ENTER MISS MERCIER!

FOR the next few days it rained most of the time, and Jesanne was made free of the Dragon House, and wandered all over it, accompanied by the dogs, learning to know it and many of its traditions, though Sir Ambrose withheld some which must come at their proper season.

An old house and an old family are generally rich in legend and family custom, and the Dragon House and the Gellibrands were exceptionally so. Sir Ambrose found it vastly interesting to have a keen fourteen-year-old to enlighten, and, though strictly to himself, of course, was moved to wish that he had left the question of a governess for the child alone, at any rate till after Christmas. He felt that once Miss Mercier, the lady he had engaged, should come, Jesanne would be lost to him, for the mornings at least, and he would miss her sorely.

As for Jesanne herself, she set all such disagreeable questions aside, and enjoyed the present. Her great wish was to find the whereabouts of the old staircase; or if not that, then the place where it *had* been. In the afternoons, when her old cousin was in the library, busy with the thousand and one details connected with a big estate, she was prowling about here, there, and everywhere, trying to find it. The letters she sent out to New Zealand were full of it; and Miss Mortimer, in her lonely home in Invercargill, became as interested in the question as her niece.

When Jesanne had been at the Dragon House five days, the weather cleared, and Sir Ambrose, after learning that she could ride, presented her with a beautiful chestnut pony, and the pair rode everywhere.

Particularly did she beg to be shown the distant entrance to the secret tunnel, and they spent a whole day riding thither and back, and having their lunch picnic-fashion in a narrow gully, where the Ddwyvyll moaned eerily over the stones in its bed, and the rocks were almost unclothed save with moss and lichens.

'It's a very frightening place,' commented Jesanne as they rode homewards, picking their way carefully among the boulders which strewed the valley. 'Why is it so bare, Cousin Ambrose?'

'The story goes that there's a curse on it,' he replied. 'Be careful, Jesanne! Keep Rufa on a tight rein just here. This isn't the best place for a frisky pony.'

Jesanne nodded. Rufa, her pony, was a handful, spirited and self-willed, though there was not an ounce of real vice in her. Luckily, the child had learnt to ride in New Zealand, and was able to handle the beautiful creature easily. They finally quitted the gloomy place and came into a heavily rutted lane down which they trotted gaily, while Sir Ambrose told his young cousin the story of the gully.

'It is said that during the priest-hunting times one Ivor Gellibrand was a priest. He came to his father's house to fulfil his office, and a distant cousin, who hated him, and hoped for the reversion of the estate if he could only get sufficient evidence against the family to bring about its sequestration, spied on him. He got the evidence he wanted—or so the story goes. But he wanted also to make sure of the place. So he resolved to take Ivor prisoner himself. He tracked him up to that lonely place when the priest left the Dragon House to go to another family of recusants, as they were called, and coming up with him, called on him to give himself up. Ivor refused, and the false cousin killed him with his dagger. Meanwhile, however, a favourite dog of the boy's—he was little more—had also followed, coming up with the pair just as Cousin Llewellyn stabbed Ivor. The dog fell on Llewellyn and killed him, and old Sir Balthazar, coming this way four days later, found the two bodies, and the dog, almost spent, lying on the body of his young master. They found papers on Llewellyn which explained plainly enough what had happened, and Sir Balthazar cursed all Llewellyn's family, and the place where the murder had taken place.'

'I don't wonder,' said Jesanne. 'What a pig that Llewellyn was! And what about the dear dog, Cousin Ambrose?'

'He died—they said of a broken heart,' replied Sir Ambrose briefly. 'He is buried outside the wall of the churchyard. I'll show you the place some day when we go that way.'

'And did the curse take effect?'

'Yes; or so it's said. At any rate, no green has ever grown in the place since. There were trees there, but a landslide tore them down a year later, and it's always been as you saw it. It's called the Valley of the Curse to this day; and the country folk wouldn't go near it after dark for all the wealth in the kingdom. Of course, Llewellyn is said to walk, though not Ivor, who is believed to have died forgiving his murderer with his last breath.'

'And what about Llewellyn's family?' asked Jesanne breathlessly.

'There were only his father and two brothers. There's no such thing as any man being able to curse another with evil. But it is a queer coincidence that during the three years which followed, that branch of the family became extinct.'

'Oh!' Jesanne thrilled to it. For once, she had almost got her fill of romance.

The next day, a letter came for Sir Ambrose which made his face turn gloomy. He looked across the table at Jesanne, who was eating porridge, serenely unaware that her days of freedom were numbered.

'Jesanne!' he said.

'Yes, Cousin Ambrose?'

'This is from Miss Mercier—the lady of whom I told you, who is coming to be your governess.'

Jesanne's face fell. 'Oh? What does she say?' Then, hopefully, 'Isn't she coming after all?'

'She is coming tomorrow. She will reach Wyesford at five in the afternoon, so I must send in the car to meet her. Do you want to go with it?'

'Oh, please, Cousin Ambrose, must I? I mean, I'd so much rather not. Are you going?'

He shook his head. 'I can't possibly. Jennings is coming up at two to see me about those cottages I told you about, that need reroofing. I don't suppose we shall finish till after four, for there is a good deal to see to. Mr Robins, my lawyer, is coming out too, as there are some leases to renew. I was going to tell you, and ask what you would like to do, as I shall be occupied until tea-time. Don't you think you had better go? It will be something to occupy you.'

'I'll go if you wish me to,' said Jesanne. 'But—but I'd much rather not.'

He considered. 'It would depend a good deal on the weather, of course. It's fine enough today. But if the rain came back—and the wind is backing towards the south-west, Carver tells me—I certainly should not wish it. Suppose we leave it at that. If it is fine, you will go. If not, I will send Hiles with the car, and we will receive Miss Mercier here.'

Jesanne agreed to this, and she prayed hard that it might be wet. They spent the last day in a wild gallop round the boundaries of the estate in the morning, while the afternoon was given up to a long walk with the four house-dogs. In the evening, Sir Ambrose began to teach Jesanne to play chess, and they were so interested in their game that it was long after ten when they finally finished.

'We'll have another gallop tomorrow morning if it's good weather,' said Sir Ambrose, as he replaced the chessmen in their box. 'If not, we'll think of something else to do. Now run along to bed. Tell Agnes to bring you some milk and biscuits if you are hungry. Good night, child.'

Jesanne said good-night, and went off, her mind divided on the question of the weather. If it were fine, she would get her gallop, but she would have to go into Wyesford, the nearest town, to meet Miss Mercier, and she did not want to do that. If it were wet, she would be saved the trip; but on the other hand, there would be no ride.

As it happened, Fate was kind to her. The morning dawned brilliantly fine, and Sir Ambrose took her off immediately after breakfast, and they had a good long ride, getting home to lunch at about half-past one. He had to go to the library for his business as soon as the meal was ended, and Jesanne went up to the schoolroom, thinking ruefully of having to meet an utter stranger by herself. At half-past two the sun was still shining; but at three the sky became overcast, and by four o'clock it was pouring with rain as it had done the day on which she had come to the Dragon House.

Jesanne gave a joyful exclamation when she saw it, and heard the beat of the storm against the windows. 'Hurrah! Now I can't go! I *am* glad!'

However, she had sufficient conscience to go and see if the rooms prepared for Miss Mercier in the north wing were all ready, with fires blazing on the hearths, and flowers set about. She also asked Agnes to have tea ready, so that the governess might have it as soon as she came. Then Totton arrived, to say that

Sir Ambrose wished Miss Gellibrand to come down to the library to pour out tea for himself and the others, so she ran off, thinking joyously that she needn't even wait to have the meal with her new governess.

Mr Jennings was an old acquaintance now, and she liked him. He was the seventh generation of his family to act as agent for the Gellibrands, and he lived with his pretty wife in the little Manor House which Nicholas Gellibrand had built when he had married Loveday Penwarne. They were childless, their only girl having died when she was six months old; and the fact that if little Edris had lived she would have been just the age of Jesanne, made them take a great interest in the heiress of the Dragon House.

Mr Robins was a tall, soldierly-looking man in the sixties, who had a grown-up family of seven and was well accustomed to girls. He speedily made friends with Jesanne, and she thoroughly enjoyed sitting behind the big silver teapot, pouring out for them, and eating the delicious cakes which Cook sent in.

But when tea was over, and the two departed, five o'clock struck, and Sir Ambrose and Jesanne looked ruefully at each other. In three-quarters of an hour at most the invader would be on them, and neither liked the prospect.

'You don't begin lessons till Monday,' said Sir Ambrose as consolingly as he could. 'I've decided that this afternoon.'

Jesanne began to giggle. 'And this is Wednesday! Miss Mercier will wonder why she's come so soon.'

'Never mind. Monday is quite soon enough. I don't want you to be a learned woman—there's no need for it. So long as you know something about the literature of your country, can speak French, write a decent letter, and cast up accounts, I shan't worry about too many frills. You don't play the piano, I think?'

Jesanne shook her head. 'No; but I've got a 'cello.'

He smiled. 'I'm afraid Miss Mercier can't teach you that. She said in her letters that she played the piano. But you don't want to learn that, eh?'

'I'd rather go on with my 'cello, please. I meant to ask you about lessons, but I've forgotten till now.'

'You have your 'cello with you?'

'Oh, yes; it was in the big wooden case with my books and some other things. Auntie Anne thought it would travel most safely that way. And, of course, it was in its own wooden case too. It's quite all right. I was trying it yesterday.'

'Well, for 'cello I'm afraid we must send over to Birmingham,' he said. 'I might send you in the car—once a fortnight, perhaps. It will mean being away all day, you see.'

'Take me yourself,' coaxed Jesanne. 'The lesson wouldn't be longer than an hour at most, and then we could have some fun.'

'We'll see. If you wish to continue, you certainly shall.'

'Oh, thank you so much! I do love my 'cello!'

'You must bring it down to the drawing-room one night and let me hear you. I've had the piano put into full order. I dare say your governess can play your accompaniments.'

'Give me time to get into practice. I haven't touched it, except for trying it last night to see how it had travelled, for six weeks or more. You do so easily get out, you know.'

He laughed. 'Very well. I'll find out who is the best master, and you shall begin your lessons after Christmas. It isn't much use starting so late this term. We are into the second week in November now. In the meantime, you can practise at what music you have.'

'Thank you, Cousin Ambrose. I'll work hard. I do really want to play well.'

'Gellibrand-like! None of us care to work at anything we can't do well. I'm glad to see it coming out in you.'

But Jesanne had something else to ask him. 'Cousin Ambrose,

I can go on with Latin, can't I? I've done a good deal—Daddy started me when I was seven, and I love it.'

He looked dubious. 'I don't know if Miss Mercier can teach Latin.'

'But ask her. If she can't, isn't there someone else who could? Couldn't *you*?'

'I'm afraid my Latin has gone beyond recovery. It is years since I touched it. Do you really want to go on with it?'

'Please,' she coaxed. 'I know I couldn't do science, though I loved it too. But I'd only had one year of it. Latin I've done for seven years. Daddy was so keen on it, you see. He said everyone should learn it, for so many other languages are based on it.'

'Well, I'll see. I certainly couldn't undertake to teach you myself. Perhaps the Rector could manage it. I'll ask him.'

Jesanne beamed. 'That will be splendid!'

'And—and you'll do your best for this lady who's coming, won't you?' asked Sir Ambrose. 'I'm sure she will be a nice companion for you. And a girl needs a woman to take care of her.'

Jesanne said nothing. If she had dared, she would have suggested that the companion she wanted was her aunt. But though she and Sir Ambrose had made great strides in friendship since that first night, she felt instinctively that he would never listen to such an idea.

'I wish he just *knew* Auntie Anne,' she thought. 'He'd love her if he did. No one could help it.'

But he was asking her which of the great classic authors she had read, and in comparing notes as to the love of both for Dickens, their liking for only certain of the Scott novels, and Jesanne's distaste for Jane Austen (though she told him that she loved *Jane Eyre* and liked *Villette*), the time passed so quickly that they were amazed to hear the sound of the car coming up the avenue.

'Better go to meet her,' said the master of the house, rising and going to the door. 'Come along, Jesanne. We must show the lady some civility.'

Jesanne followed him nervously. She felt rather as if she were going into the dentist's surgery. Except for what she had read in books, she knew nothing of private governesses. What would Miss Mercier be like?

Three minutes later, the lady was descending from the car, and Sir Ambrose was going forward with stately courtesy to greet her, asking if she had had a pleasant journey, and if Hiles, the chauffeur, had found her quickly.

'Quite pleasant, thank you,' was the answer in a rather hard, clear-cut voice. 'And the chauffeur found me almost at once.'

'Ah! I am glad of that. But you must be very cold after a journey on such an afternoon, and with a fourteen miles' drive at the end of it. Come into the library and warm yourself, and then Jesanne shall take you upstairs and show you your rooms.'

'Thank you; that will be very nice. But there is quite a good fire here,' replied Miss Mercier with an appreciative glance at the great logs burning on the dogs on the hearth.

'True; but this is rather a draughty place without the screens, and we have not yet put them up. Totton must see about it tomorrow.—Jesanne, my dear, here is Miss Mercier.'

Jesanne came reluctantly forward, and held out her hand, which the lady took limply. 'So this is—what did you say, Sir Ambrose?—Jesanne? Not an English name, surely?'

'Oh, yes; quite English,' said Jesanne as politely as she could, considering that she felt rather like a cat rubbed up the wrong way. Everyone seemed so surprised at her name. She *did* wish people would take it for granted, and not go on commenting on it.

Miss Mercier laughed, a little, chilly laugh. 'Oh, indeed? I never heard it before. It is certainly uncommon.'

Sir Ambrose intervened. 'Come along to the library.— Jesanne, you are shivering in this draughty place. Make haste, dear. I don't want you to catch cold.'

They left the hall, and went to the library, where he pushed a chair invitingly before the great blaze, and the lady sat down. While she plied her host with remarks, Jesanne, from her own corner, observed her closely. She saw a tall, elegant-looking woman, handsome in rather a hard style. Her eyes were cold and grey; her lips shut firmly over strong white teeth; under the smart hat, what could be seen of her hair was grey, and carefully dressed. She was middle-aged, and looked every year of her age. Jesanne felt that she would be no mean adversary if it ever came to war between them. She hoped it would not. Cousin Ambrose was certainly showing himself much kinder than she had ever suspected he could be, and she wanted to please him if she could. Then she suddenly woke up to the fact that Miss Mercier was speaking to her.

'And so you are Jesanne? Well, I hope that we shall soon be good friends, and work happily together.'

'Oh, I expect you will,' said Sir Ambrose. 'Now, if you are quite sure you are warm, Jesanne will take you up to your rooms. I think she has tea waiting for you.'

'Yes, Cousin Ambrose,' said Jesanne. 'I told Agnes to have it ready in my sitting-room.'

'That was right. We dine at eight, Miss Mercier, but I think you would like a cup of tea now.'

'Thank you. It would certainly be refreshing,' agreed Miss Mercier, rising and gathering up the furs she had laid aside.

Jesanne led the way from the library, up the old stairs, and along the corridor to the north wing. She opened a door, and Miss Mercier walked in, and looked appreciatively about the comfortable place with its log fire, handsome Georgian furniture, and pretty hangings.

'What a very pleasant room!' she said. 'And this door—does it lead into your room?'

'Oh, no,' said Jesanne, opening it. 'This is your sitting-room. Cousin Ambrose thought you would prefer to have your own. My rooms are in the other wing.'

Miss Mercier's smile faded. 'Oh indeed? I expected you were to be entirely under my care, and I like my pupils close at hand, even at night. I must speak to Sir Ambrose about it tomorrow. It is so much better, my dear. In case of illness, I could then look after you quite easily.'

'But I am never ill,' replied Jesanne. 'And Cousin Ambrose arranged for me to be near him. His suite is next door to mine.'

Miss Mercier was wise enough to let the subject drop. She removed her hat and coat, and changed her shoes for pretty slippers. Then she suggested that she would like to have her tea, and also see Jesanne's rooms. Jesanne agreed, and led the way to her own pretty quarters.

'Cousin Ambrose thought we might use my sitting-room as the schoolroom for the present,' she explained as they crossed at the back of the Angel Gallery and went down the corridor to the south wing. 'I think, though, that he is going to have one of the downstairs rooms arranged for us after Christmas.'

Agnes was just going out of the sitting-room as they reached it. She stood aside to let them pass, and Jesanne said, 'Please bring the tea, Agnes, will you?' before she followed her governess into the room.

Miss Mercier stood looking round with approval until her eyes fell on Sanchia, curled up asleep in her basket in a dark corner. Then she turned and said sharply, 'A dog? Yours, my dear?'

'Yes,' said Jesanne. 'Sanchia is my own little pet. Isn't she sweet?'

Miss Mercier evaded the question, commenting frigidly,

'Surely she doesn't live up here? She is in the kitchen most of the time, I hope.'

'Oh, no,' said Jesanne innocently. 'She is up here except when she goes for her runs. At night, her basket is put in a far corner of my room.'

'Oh, my dear, I don't think we can permit that! It is most unhealthy!'

'But it is such a large room,' explained Jesanne. 'See!' And she threw open the connecting door to show her bedroom. The lamp was turned down, so she went in and turned it up, and Miss Mercier entered and looked disapprovingly round the great chamber with its three long, wide windows, reaching nearly to the floor, its glowing fire, and all the dainty appointments, which were certainly unusually luxurious for a schoolgirl.

'Yes; I see. But all the same, I'm afraid I can't allow you to have a dog in your sleeping-apartment. I must speak to Sir Ambrose about it. Men don't think about these things, my dear. Your little dog will be very comfortable in the kitchens, I am sure. We will ask Cook to see that her basket is in a nice corner where there are no draughts, and she will soon get used to it and be quite happy. But I can't permit dogs either here or in the schoolroom.'

Jesanne looked at her curiously, but said nothing. For one thing, she was indignant at this calm taking possession of her and her belongings, and was rather afraid of what might happen if she spoke. All the same, she made up her mind that she would not let Sanchia go without a struggle.

Miss Mercier continued looking round the large room—larger, by far, than even her own spacious quarters, as she did not fail to notice—with growing disapprobation. She considered that such a place and such appointments were absurd for a mere schoolgirl. Jesanne ought to be in a small room, if not opening out of hers, at least next to it, where she could keep an oversight of all her doings.

'Well,' she said at length, 'I expect the maid has brought up the tea, so perhaps we had better go back to the schoolroom. I am sure you are hungry.'

'I've had my tea, thank you,' replied Jesanne politely.

'You didn't wait for me, then?'

'Cousin Ambrose sent for me to pour out tea for some people he had with him,' explained the child.

'Oh, I see. Well, come along.'

Jesanne paused only to turn down the lamp again, and then followed the lady into the sitting-room, where a dainty tea-table had been placed beside the fire. Miss Mercier sat down, and then turned to Agnes, who was just leaving the room.

'You are the schoolroom maid, I believe? What is your name?'

'Agnes, ma'am,' replied Agnes.

'Ah! Well, when you prepare Miss Jesanne's room for the night, I wish you to take her dog down to the kitchens. I expect Cook can find some safe corner for it there.'

Agnes turned a dismayed look on Jesanne, who sat bolt upright in her chair, her cheeks scarlet with sudden anger.

'I—I'm afraid I can't do that, ma'am,' stammered the maid. 'Cook don't allow no dogs in the kitchens. Even old Beowulf ain't—isn't allowed there. And the cats would kill the puppy, too. Gipsy has kittens.'

Miss Mercier's eyes hardened. She looked at Agnes with a kind of haughty surprise. 'Indeed? Well, I must speak to Cook myself. At any rate, the dog will not stay up here. I permit no pets in my schoolroom.'

Jesanne opened her lips to retort. Then she shut them again. She had made up her mind to give the governess no chance to complain of her behaviour if it could be helped. As for Agnes, she looked positively bewildered.

'Cook won't hear of it, ma'am,' she said civilly. 'And

Sir Ambrose always says that Sanchia is Miss Gellibrand's dog, and must be under her care.'

At this point, Sanchia, who had been sleeping the sleep of the healthily tired puppy, stirred, and sat up. She decided that she would join the company, so she leaped from her basket, bounded at Jesanne, who tried to catch her, and then wriggled away to sniff at Miss Mercier. She was the friendliest pup in the world, and expected everyone to be her friend; so she got a nasty surprise when the governess gave a little scream and pushed her roughly aside.

'Go away! Get away! Agnes, take this animal downstairs at once! She is not to be allowed to come up here! I won't permit it!'

Jesanne sprang forward and caught her pet away, her eyes blazing with fury. 'Sanchia is *my* dog, Miss Mercier, and she *must* stay with me. Cousin Ambrose says so!'

Miss Mercier, however, had unfortunately caught a good deal of the silly Alsatianphobia, and she was honestly afraid of all Alsatians.

'She will do no such thing! In any case, nothing would induce me to have an Alsatian near me! Nasty treacherous things! I shall tell Sir Ambrose so, and insist that she must be got rid of!' she cried unguardedly.

Jesanne nearly choked with rage. Then she controlled herself, and said as quietly as she could, 'It's a mistake to think that of Alsatians. Cousin Ambrose says so, and he ought to know, for there are seventeen at the kennels, besides Donna and Storm who live in the house. And *far* worse than any Alsatian is Beowulf, my cousin's mastiff. He doesn't like strangers, partly because he's old, Cousin Ambrose says. Even I had to be specially introduced to him. He's a darling when you know him.' Then she added earnestly, 'Please don't try to push him when you meet him. He mightn't like it.'

Agnes took advantage of this speech to vanish with her tray, and Miss Mercier was so overcome at this last piece of information that she never noticed the departure of the maid.

'What?' she exclaimed. 'Do you mean to say that full-grown Alsatians are allowed to roam about the house?'

'Oh, yes,' said Jesanne, too much a Gellibrand to understand that the lady was really terrified of all big dogs. 'They have beautiful manners, though they are mischievous, of course. And they are beauties too. Why, Storm already has one Championship certificate. They're away at a big show today, or you would have seen them. And I think Beowulf must have been at the kennels when you came. I expect he'll be downstairs now. Shall I show you the way back to your rooms as you have finished tea? Then I must change for dinner before I run down to ask what we've done at the show.'

But Miss Mercier had a new grievance. 'Surely a child like you does not come in to dinner?' she exclaimed. 'Why, you ought to go to bed at half-past eight!'

Jesanne opened her eyes. 'Of course I come in to dinner! I'm fourteen—not a baby.' She turned down the lamp as she spoke, Sir Ambrose having impressed on her that she must never leave a lamp burning full when she left a room.

Miss Mercier followed her back to her own quarters, where Jesanne left the lady, tore back to her own room to change in double-quick time, and then raced downstairs so wildly that she caught her foot and rolled down the last half-dozen steps. She picked herself up before Totton, who was in the hall overseeing the setting up of the screens to mask the draughts from the great door, could even exclaim, and made for the library, where Sir Ambrose, with a very rueful face, was examining the certificates Carver had just left with him.

He looked up, startled, as his young cousin literally tumbled into the room, cheeks flaming, eyes sparkling, hair all ruffled as the result of her swift flight through the house, and her tumble.

'Hello!' he said. 'What's the matter?'

'Cousin Ambrose,' cried Jesanne, 'that's a *horrid* woman! She wants to send my Sanchia to the kitchens, and she hates dogs, and she thinks I ought to go to bed at half-past eight and not come in to dinner! And I'll never like her— *never*!'

Chapter VII

AN UNPLEASANT DILEMMA

Sir Ambrose was really very much upset. He wished that he had never heard the word 'governess,' much less seen one of the tribe. At the same time, he could scarcely dismiss the lady at once because she did not like dogs. But what was going to happen was more than he could see. He listened in troubled silence while Jesanne poured forth her tale, and then remained silent for another minute or two, thinking hard.

'Sanchia will certainly remain with you,' he said at length. 'You have assumed the responsibility of her, and I shall not permit you to cast off any responsibility you have assumed of your own free will unless it is bad for your health. But the pup is yours, and you have to see to her training. I will speak to Miss Mercier about it, and tell her it is my wish that she remains with you. At the same time, you must see that the pup doesn't annoy your governess.'

'*That* won't be easy,' said Jesanne ruefully. 'She hates all dogs. Oh, Cousin Ambrose, can't you send her away and get someone else who likes them?'

'No,' he said curtly. 'That would be most unfair to Miss Mercier. We'll have to put up with it. And perhaps she may learn to like them,' he added hopefully.

'It would take an earthquake to do that,' said Jesanne, not hopeful in the least. 'And if she's scared of my Sanchia, what *will* she be like with Donna and Storm?'

Sir Ambrose sighed. Plainly it was not going to be easy, this having a small girl in the house, along with her governess.

'We must see that they don't tease her,' he said. 'And we must remember, Jesanne, that Miss Mercier is a stranger under our roof, and that Gellibrands treat strangers courteously.'

The sound of steps on the stairs brought him to his feet, and he looked at his young cousin. 'You don't look very tidy. Slip out through the office, and brush your hair, or we shall have that governess of yours talking to us.'

Jesanne put up a hand to the thick, straight hair, and discovered that it was all on end. 'I fell down the stairs,' she explained. 'No; I didn't hurt myself—not much, anyway. I'm off!' And she shot through a little hidden door into the office where Sir Ambrose was wont to transact most of the estate business, just as Miss Mercier, directed by Totton, came in at the main one.

Totton, appealed to by Jesanne as she tore past him, kept back dinner for ten minutes, thereby braving his master's wrath. But Sir Ambrose was too much perturbed to have noticed if the meal had been an hour late. Donna and Storm, now returned, were lying in their usual corners when the governess entered, and only a stern word from their master kept them in their places. They were mischievous and young, and intensely inquisitive, and they wanted to know something about this stranger who had invaded their home.

'You must meet two more members of our household, Miss Mercier,' said the inwardly-quaking head of the house. 'Here, Storm—Donna!'

Pacing in majestic style, the two Alsatians came to stand by him. Miss Mercier controlled a little shriek with difficulty. These great creatures were infinitely worse than Jesanne's puppy. But she liked her comfortable quarters; Sir Ambrose was paying her a most liberal salary; and there was only one girl to teach. Her last post had been with a family where there were three daughters, five cousins, and one friend of the daughters. Her rooms had been neither so spacious nor so luxurious as those at the Dragon House, and, apart from actual lessons, she had been obliged to give a great deal of oversight to the children's playtime. Here, she had been explicitly told that, unless she wished to have Jesanne with her, her hours would be from nine to four. After that, she might consider her time as her own. The dogs were a serious drawback, but she felt that she must just put up with them.

So when Sir Ambrose gravely introduced the picked pair to her, she admired their beautiful heads and coats, and even contrived to pat Storm between the ears. And Storm twitched his ears, and looked sidewise at his sister, saying, 'H'm! Scared to death of us! We must see about this!' For it is a fact that dogs at once sense any fear of them, and, from sheer mischief, will play on those fears.

'I did not know you were all such dog-lovers, Sir Ambrose,' said Miss Mercier when at length they were seated round the table in the dining-room.

'A Gellibrand trait,' replied Sir Ambrose, waving away Totton's offer of wine. 'The Gellibrand kennels have been well known for many generations now. I am glad to see,' he added levelly, 'that my young cousin inherits the love along with a good many other Gellibrand characteristics.'

Miss Mercier had no means of knowing that Jesanne had been in the library before her own entrance, for the young lady had been waiting demurely in the hall when the moaning of the gong called them to dinner. So she said, 'Yes; I have noticed it already. But, dear Sir Ambrose, I am going to ask you as a favour to have her puppy kept out of the schoolroom during lesson hours. I find,' she went on serenely, while Totton removed the soup-plates with an impassive face that covered many emotions, 'that pets in the schoolroom are apt to distract the attention.'

'Of course, during lessons the pup must be with the other house-dogs,' said Sir Ambrose, with a warning glance at Jesanne, who had gone pink. 'But once they are over, Jesanne will have Sanchia with her as she does now. She is responsible for the pup's well-being, and unless she is actually engaged in schoolwork, must be ready to give her proper oversight.'

It was Miss Mercier's turn to go pink. Already she knew that lessons were to occupy only the morning hours. Sir Ambrose had a horror of what he called 'blue-stockings,' and while he wished his heiress to come up to the standard of other girls, he had no desire that she should become a learned woman. From what he had just said, the governess realised that the puppy would certainly be in the schoolroom in the afternoons, even though she might be banished in the mornings. It was a predicament. However, she had an overweening confidence in her own ability to get what she wanted in the long run; so she determined to make the best of a bad job, and leave it to time to enable her to oust Sanchia altogether.

The subject was changed, Sir Ambrose speaking of the beauties of the country, and for the rest of dinner they talked on general subjects.

After dinner, Jesanne, previously instructed by her cousin, led the way into the drawing-room, which had been rescued from its former status of holland covers and dust-sheets, and was now blazing with light, and warm with a crackling fire of oak and applewood. Miss Mercier sniffed the fragrant smoke, and felt better. Perhaps she had been a little premature in trying to interfere with her pupil's dog quite so soon. She felt sure that this would prove a post after her own heart, so it behoved her to make friends with the girl. She sat down by the fire, stretching out a well-shod and pretty foot to the blaze, and called Jesanne to her side.

'Jesanne, my dear, bring that low chair and come and sit beside me. It will soon be your bedtime, and we must get to know each other a little first, must we not?'

On her very best behaviour, Jesanne brought the chair and sat down, folding her hands in her lap.

'Have you no needlework?' asked her governess.

'No; I don't like sewing,' returned Jesanne.

'That is a pity. However, next week we will make an expedition to the town and get you some embroidery. It will give you something to do during this hour each night.'

'Cousin Ambrose generally likes to play games,' explained Jesanne. 'He has a letter to write for Hiles to take into Wyesford to post, or he would have been here now.'

'Oh, I expect he will be quite glad to be relieved from childish games every night,' said Miss Mercier suavely. 'And every gentlewoman should know how to use her needle.'

Now Miss Anne Mortimer had drilled this well into her niece; and much as Jesanne disliked needlework, she was quite good at it, for she had been well taught. But hearing the remark from her governess's lips was almost more than the child could bear. And as for childish games—

'Cousin Ambrose has been teaching me to play chess,' she said in her curiously deep voice. 'And we sometimes play cribbage and écarté.'

'Still, at your age, there is so much to learn that I think we must dedicate this hour to sewing each night. And now, tell me, what is your favourite lesson?'

Jesanne eyed the lady for a moment. Then, 'Latin and 'cello,' she said sweetly.

She was not disappointed. Miss Mercier's face fell. 'Latin? Oh, my dear, I am sorry to hear that. Latin is essential for boys, of course; but I cannot think it necessary for a girl in your position. But you cannot have gone very far in it yet?'

'We were doing the *Aeneid* at school when I left,' said Jesanne briskly. 'Fourth book. And Caesar, of course. I've learnt Latin for years.'

'My dear child, you mustn't exaggerate. That is most unladylike. I suppose you began two years ago? You cannot call two years "years" in the sense you did.'

'I didn't. I began Latin when I was seven. My father taught me.'

This was worse than Miss Mercier had expected. 'But surely you like other lessons? And what about the piano?'

'I stopped learning that when I was eight. I've had a 'cello ever since then. But Cousin Ambrose says I must go to Birmingham for lessons,' explained Jesanne blandly.

Now Miss Mercier disliked the 'cello. She was—justly—proud of her musical abilities, and her execution on the piano was excellent. She had a hard, clear touch, and if her playing was rather mechanical, it was both accurate and brilliant. She had always done well with music pupils, and it was a bitter disappointment to learn that her new pupil was unlikely to add to her successes.

'But surely you will take it up again now,' she said. 'Two hours' practice a day would soon make a difference in your playing. I think I must speak to Sir Ambrose about it. And then you can give an hour to the 'cello. The piano is really much more useful to a girl than the 'cello.'

Indignation kept Jesanne silent, which was just as well, for there might have been a nasty explosion otherwise. And, mercifully, Sir Ambrose, having finished his letter and sent Hiles off in the car with it, came into the drawing-room at that moment.

'An important letter that had to go at once,' he explained, apologising to Miss Mercier for leaving her alone. 'Still, I expect Jesanne has been able to entertain you.'

'We have been having a little chat, learning to know one another,' said Miss Mercier sweetly. 'But I must see that Jesanne has some needlework for the evenings. Perhaps next week you could send us into the nearest town, and then we could choose something pretty.'

Now, as it happened, Sir Ambrose was one of the men who objected to seeing his womenfolk absorbed in needlework in the evenings. He had a theory that working by artificial light was a strain on the eyes. And, apart from that, he enjoyed his evening games with his young cousin, and was not minded to lose them. So he only looked very blank, and said he would be unable to make any arrangements for the present.

Then he turned to Jesanne.

'A fine moonlight night, after all the rain. Jesanne, if you like to wrap up and put on thick boots, you may bring Sanchia and come with me when I take the dogs for their walk. Perhaps Miss Mercier would join us?' He turned courteously to the lady.

Miss Mercier emphatically would *not*. She was the kind of person who considered moonlight walks silly, and she was far too comfortable by the fire to like the idea of leaving her comfortable chair and sallying forth into the sharp chill of a November night. She declined the invitation, and even hinted that she thought Jesanne ought to be thinking of going to bed instead of taking a moonlight stroll. She mentioned the hour and the chilliness of the weather, and suggested that nine o'clock ought to be bedtime for a fourteen-year-old.

Sir Ambrose laughed pleasantly, and brushed her hints aside. Jesanne would be back in plenty of time for half-past nine bedtime. She was a healthy girl, accustomed to the sharpness of winter in Invercargill, in New Zealand, where she had lived during the past four years. Any girl who knew the icy South Polar winds that sweep across the desolate Southern Ocean unhindered by any stretches of land-masses ought to be able to withstand such sharp weather as the western counties of England can show.

He sent the child to her room, charging her to tell Agnes to be ready for her at twenty-past nine; and then, after making certain that the governess knew her way back to her own rooms, suggested that she would find them all ready for her, with good fires, and the newest books and magazines. If she wanted tea or coffee, she had only to ring and ask.

Miss Mercier gave way of necessity, and departed, inwardly determined that night walks should cease to be a part of Jesanne's life as soon as she could manage it. She foresaw that she must walk warily, but she had never yet failed when she had undertaken to bring a recalcitrant parent or guardian to seeing with her eyes.

Once she had gone, Sir Ambrose went to bring Beowulf from the library where he had been enjoying a quiet snooze, and summon Donna and Storm from the hall. He called up the stairs, and presently Jesanne came dancing down in her warm coat and cap, her hands in thick gloves, her feet in equally thick boots, a scarf muffled round her throat, and Sanchia leaping down the stairs in advance.

'Come along!' he said. 'We must get off, or we shall have that governess of yours on our track. I see she means to be strict with you.'

'She'll get over that presently,' said Jesanne comfortably as she followed him out into the clear November moonlight. 'Oh, what a glorious night! Look, Cousin Ambrose! There's a falling star! Another soul has gone to Heaven!'

He glanced up at the deep blue velvet of the skies, where the stars powdered the darkness with silver frosting. 'Yes; November is the meteor month. Do you know the names of the stars and constellations? Look; there's old Orion with Sirius. And that's the Plough. See the Milky Way.'

Jesanne looked up eagerly. Her father had taught her the names of the principal constellations of the New Zealand skies, and she wanted to learn those of English skies. Sir Ambrose was pleased to find that she listened to him with interest, and was quick to pick out the constellations as he pointed them out.

'Where now?' she asked, when at length he said they must be getting off, or they would have no walk.

'Straight down the drive,' he replied. 'We'll turn at the Three Oaks, and come round by Raphael's path. That'll give the dogs a good breather, and get you back by half-past nine with any luck. Come along!'

They set off, the dogs galloping ahead like mad things, and Sanchia lolloping after them. In the white light everything looked more clean-cut than usual, and there was a weird beauty about the landscape that thrilled Jesanne. Right ahead lay the Black Mountains of Wales, grim and austere, heaving heavy shoulders against the deep blue of the starry sky. Behind lay the great mass of the old house, with the lights twinkling from its windows here and there. In the distance other lights, of farm and cottage, gleamed through the darkness. To the left ran the singing waters of the Ddwyvyll. Jesanne could hear it chuckling and crooning to itself in the gloom. However much she loved New Zealand, she had to confess that this place had a magic lure all its own. She gave herself a little hug of pure joy, and then turned to her cousin.

'How lovely it all is! I don't wonder old Balthazar chose to build his house here!'

Sir Ambrose laughed. 'He'd never recognise the place if he could come back to it now.'

'Why not?' asked Jesanne.

'Because in his time it was mainly forest round here,' explained her cousin. 'Practically the whole countryside was covered with a great forest of beech and oak. Balthazar cleared only enough to give him the site and a space round the house. The rest has been done since then. Why, even I can remember when the Dragon

House was far more isolated than it now is. In his time it must have been a very lonely spot.'

'Perhaps that's why he chose it,' suggested Jesanne.

'It may be. At any rate, he liked it. And his bride seems to have been happy enough.'

"I think I can understand that,' said Jesanne thoughtfully. 'I shall always love New Zealand best. It's my own country, you see. But no one could help loving this part of the world too. I *must*, I suppose, because my ancestors came from here. But even a stranger would have to love it—it *gets* you, somehow.'

Her cousin nodded. 'Yes; that's true. It's good hearing to me, little maid. We shall not quarrel because you love your birthplace best. But I am glad that old England means something to you as well.'

'Oh, but it means a lot to everyone in the Empire,' said Jesanne quickly. 'Daddy used to say that it was like a tree. The Empire is the branches, but all the branches draw their life-sap from the main stem.'

Again he nodded. 'Yes; that also is true. One tree, with many branches—but, one tree.'

They had reached Three Oaks by this time. It was a small glade where three great oaks, all reputed to be of great age, dating from centuries before Master Gellibrand ever laid the foundations of his Dragon House, stood by themselves. They were so old that some of the branches had been propped, and the main trunks were carefully stayed against the force of the winter storms. Young beeches and other oaks were planted at a distance round to break the force of the fierce gales that came leaping down the narrow valleys in the autumn and spring. Gellibrands were proud of Three Oaks.

Jesanne paused to look at them. 'I wonder what tales they could tell if they could speak?' she murmured.

'Many, no doubt,' replied Sir Ambrose. 'A duel took place there between Gellibrand brothers. It was there that Caspar Gellibrand hid for one whole night and day before he got into the Dragon House. This one,' he laid his hand on a noble veteran, 'is quite hollow. Caspar knew it, and he climbed the tree and dropped down inside. It cannot have been comfortable, but it was better than a gallows on Hangman's Mound, which was the alternative.'

'I thought they sent people to the Tower in those days,' said Jesanne.

He smiled slightly. 'Only the leaders. For such as Caspar Gellibrand, it would have been short shrift and a rope.'

Jesanne shuddered. 'How horrible! I'm glad, after all, I didn't live in those days.'

'Yes; they were brutal days—the days of the witch trials, and hanging for a starving man who snatched a loaf of bread. They are well past, thank God. Now we must turn, or you won't be in bed by ten, and your governess will come down on us both.'

'She's going to be an awful trial,' sighed Jesanne, as she turned to hunt for Sanchia. '—Oh, the dogs must have put up a rabbit! Listen to them!'

And indeed there was a furious yelling which reached even Miss Mercier, sitting at ease in her comfortable sitting-room, glancing over one or two of the latest weeklies, and toasting her toes before the sweet-smelling wood fire. She shivered as she heard the sound, and putting down her magazine, fell to pondering how she would manage in this house of dog-fiends.

It dawned on her that Jesanne had either not come in yet, or else had skipped off to bed without coming to bid her good-night. Either was most undesirable. She felt that she really must speak to Sir Ambrose as soon as possible about the child's keeping to regular hours.

'And I will also ask him to let her have a bedroom near here,' she thought. '*He* will never know if she reads in bed at night. She ought to be next to me, and then I can keep an eye on her.'

At that moment there was a gentle rap at the door, and when she called 'Come in!' Sir Ambrose himself appeared, old Beowulf beside him, and Jesanne hanging on to his other arm.

'I've brought the truant back, Miss Mercier,' he said cheerily. 'She has come to bid you good-night, and then she must run off to bed. We are rather later than I intended, but the dogs put up a rabbit and would not come for calling. Be quick, Jesanne, and I'll take you across to Agnes. Oh, one moment, though. Miss Mercier, please give me your hand.'

Much amazed, Miss Mercier did as he asked, and he took it, saying imperatively, 'A friend, Beowulf. Good dog; a friend!' Then he released her.

'But—why?' asked the startled lady.

'I thought Jesanne had explained. Beowulf is getting old—he is thirteen in the spring—and he is apt to be suspicious of strangers. But it is all right now. He will not interfere with you. Now, Jesanne, bid good-night, and come along.'

Jesanne came forward. Under her cousin's compelling eye, she offered her hand. 'Good night, Miss Mercier,' she said. 'I hope you will sleep well, and be comfortable.'

Miss Mercier tried to draw her closer to kiss her, but Jesanne stiffened her arm, and the governess had to be content with a handshake as she said, 'Good night, Jesanne. You must make haste and get to sleep, or you will be too tired for lessons in the morning.'

'Oh, we'll see about lessons when tomorrow comes,' said Sir Ambrose hastily. 'No need to be in too big a hurry, and we must show you the lie of the land first. Run along, little maid. I'll come and say good-night in a few minutes.'

Jesanne laughed, and raced off, followed by Sanchia, who had come with her. Sir Ambrose made a few more courteous remarks to Miss Mercier, and then called Beowulf to heel, and left her, advising her to get a good rest, and telling her that her morning tea would be brought up at eight the next morning.

'We have breakfast about nine,' he said. 'Good night, Miss Mercier. If you find you have not everything you want, please ring, and someone will attend to you.'

Then he left the room, and Miss Mercier was left to reflect that she must get her new pupil in hand as speedily as possible.

Chapter VIII

LESSONS BEGIN

DESPITE all Miss Mercier's hints and, finally, open suggestions as to the necessity for not wasting time, no lessons were given that week. Sir Ambrose contrived to be free, and, in the afternoons, drove the lady and his small cousin all round the neighbourhood. In the mornings, Jesanne had orders to take her governess about the park as long as it was fine.

'Tell her some of the stories,' suggested Sir Ambrose.

'Yes; some,' agreed Jesanne. 'But not all, Cousin Ambrose. I—I somehow think she wouldn't be interested in all of them.'

'Well, use your own judgment. But whatever you feel about her, be courteous. She is our guest and employee.'

So Jesanne took the lady to Three Oaks and told her about Caspar Gellibrand. Miss Mercier made little comment. She was beginning to realise that if she wished to gain the upper hand she must be careful what she said. She had been in old houses before, and her experience had taught her to be wary of criticism.

On Sunday they attended morning service in the old parish church, which had a history dating back to the days of Edward III. Miss Mercier was enthusiastic about the beautiful Perpendicular building, and the great east window which was of very old glass. Jesanne, knowing nothing about architecture, was frankly bored during the whole of the drive back to the Dragon House, for her governess discoursed with Sir Ambrose on the subject the whole way.

'Yes; it is a very fine specimen,' he said finally. 'It was in very dilapidated condition some fifty years or so ago, but the Rector of that time was learned in archaeology, and he collected the money to have it restored, and engaged as architect a young man with the same tastes as himself. You see the result.' Then he turned to Jesanne, and added, 'And here's a story for you, Jesanne. That same Rector had a granddaughter who was a very pretty girl. Young Edmunds the architect stayed at the Rectory by the Rector's special wish, and when he finally left, he took with him not only a substantial cheque and the beginning of a great career, but a very charming wife. Their wedding was the first to be celebrated in the church after its restoration.'

'How thrilling!' said Jesanne. 'And were they happy?'

'Very happy, though it did not last so long. Mrs Edmunds lived long enough to know that her husband would go far; but she died when they had been married nine years.'

'Oh, how sad!'

'Edmunds? Is that Sir Henry Edmunds?' asked Miss Mercier.

'Yes; he is about my age, and we are old friends, though I see little of him nowadays. He went blind three years ago, you know.'

'Oh, Cousin Ambrose—*no*!' Jesanne's voice rang out in horror.

'Unfortunately, it is true. But he is a very happy man still, so you need not be miserable for him, little maid. By a strange coincidence,' he went on, turning back to Miss Mercier, 'Mr Jennings, my agent, married a granddaughter of his. Their only child, who died when she was a baby, was named "Edris" after her grandmother.'

'How old would she have been if she had lived?' asked Jesanne.

'I'm afraid I don't really know. About your age, I believe.' Then he went on, 'It was a blow to the Jennings, for she was their only child. They have never had another.'

'I wish she'd lived,' said Jesanne. 'Then she might have been a friend for me.'

THE LOST STAIRCASE

Sir Ambrose smiled. 'Never mind, Jesanne. There may be a friend for you before long. Now here we are, so jump out and catch the dogs. I see they are all ready for a wild welcome.'

In the excitement of grabbing Donna and Storm by their neck-chains to prevent them from jumping at Miss Mercier, Jesanne forgot what he had said, and in the stress of the near future it all passed completely out of her mind.

And now Monday had come, and with Monday, lessons were to begin. Jesanne thought of them apprehensively as she got up, had her bath, and got into her riding-kit. Her cousin had told her to be ready by half-past seven, and they would have a good gallop before breakfast. Jesanne tied up her hair and tucked it under her cap, caught up her little riding-crop, and went quietly along the gallery and down the stairs to the hall, where Sir Ambrose was awaiting her.

'Ready on time,' he said. 'Come along! The horses are outside.'

He saw Jesanne safely mounted, then swung himself up on the back of The Camel, a big weight-carrier, who had earned his name from his supercilious expression, and they set off at a canter down the avenue.

The noise of the hoofs on the gravel roused Miss Mercier, and she went to her window to look out, and saw the riders disappearing in the distance.

'That must stop,' she thought, as she went back to her warm bed with a shiver. 'The child will be too tired for lessons, and I shall have endless trouble with her. I must explain it fully to Sir Ambrose. A growing girl needs plenty of rest.'

But Jesanne certainly did not *look* tired when she came to breakfast in her short grey skirt, white silk blouse with big crimson bow under the collar, and her hair carefully brushed and plaited by Agnes's expert hands. Her cheeks were glowing, and her eyes were sparkling as a result of the healthy exercise in the fresh morning air, and she ate an enormous breakfast.

'I think I saw you going out on the horses before breakfast,' said Miss Mercier, addressing Sir Ambrose as he rose to help Jesanne to kidneys and bacon.

'Yes,' he said. 'We have always ridden at ten before; but now that she will be occupied with lessons at that hour, I have arranged to take her before breakfast. There you are, Jesanne. If you get through that after all the porridge you ate, you'll do well.'

Miss Mercier glanced at the loaded plate. 'Oh, Sir Ambrose!' she exclaimed. 'I hope you won't mind, but I do think that after porridge, toast and marmalade ought to be quite sufficient for a schoolgirl.'

'You don't know the kind of appetite before-breakfast exercise gives you, Miss Mercier,' he told her. 'I dare say Jesanne will be able to manage toast and marmalade when she finishes that—eh, Jesanne?'

Jesanne laughed. 'I'm ravenous,' she confessed. 'Tea or coffee, Miss Mercier?'

'Coffee, please,' replied Miss Mercier. This was another grievance with her. She did not think it right that a child of fourteen should be allowed to preside behind the urns. However, Sir Ambrose, after the period of having to pour out for himself which had succeeded the death of Rosalind, had been delighted to have Jesanne do it for him, and had refused to pay any attention to the hints of the governess.

Jesanne ministered to everyone's wants, and then fell on her breakfast with healthy gusto.

'We must begin lessons as soon after breakfast as possible,' observed Miss Mercier presently. 'It will be quite half-past nine by then, and that will not leave us much time.'

'Prayers at half-past nine,' said Sir Ambrose. 'If you start at ten and work till one, that will give you three hours, which ought to be long enough for the morning. What will you do this afternoon?'

'I really think,' said the governess, 'that we must take at least an hour of the afternoon for more lessons. Otherwise, we shall be unable to do everything.'

Sir Ambrose shook his head. 'No, Miss Mercier. I am sorry, but I never think that work done in the afternoon is good work. Jesanne will have her practice to put in, and I suppose she must do a certain amount of sewing. Then she ought to have a good walk or a romp with the dogs. All this must come in the afternoon. After Christmas, there will be her 'cello and dancing lessons. And I expect you will wish her to do a little preparation. But I am not going to allow her to overwork.'

He did not say so, but one of his reasons for this was that the delicate Rosalind had been overworked for two years by the governess he had had for the girls. It had not affected Gwen; but Rosalind had broken down, and he could never rid himself of the feeling that, had he been more observant, she need never have had the illness, and, perhaps, might have lived even when her brother went. He was resolved that no such mistakes should be made where Jesanne was concerned.

Miss Mercier looked disgusted, but already she knew better than to try to turn her employer from a course on which he was plainly set. Less than a week at the Dragon House had taught her that.

'Very well, then, Sir Ambrose,' she said. 'It must be as you decide, of course.'

'Well, after Prayers you must begin,' he said. 'I'll look in later on and see how you are getting on.'

So after Prayers, which meant at about ten to ten, Jesanne led the way upstairs to her sitting-room, where lessons were to be taken for the present, and sat down solemnly at one side of the table, while Miss Mercier took the head.

'We had better begin by going through the books you have been using,' she said. 'Please bring them here.'

Jesanne brought them from the shelves where they had been placed the night before, and laid them before her governess. Inwardly, she wondered what the lady would make of them, for already she knew that Miss Mercier's ideas of education were based on her own schooldays, while these books were modern of the modern.

Miss Mercier picked up the first, and looked at it. 'H'm! Empire history. Have you gone far in this?'

'Just up to the conquest of Canada,' said Jesanne.

'I see. What else have you done in history?'

'A general survey of the history of England—more detail when it deals with New Zealand, of course; and history of New Zealand up to the present day.'

'I see. Well, for the present, I think you had better do detailed work in English history. It is shameful for an English girl not to know the history of her own country.'

'But I am not English,' said Jesanne demurely. 'I'm a New Zealander.'

'You will be English now,' said Miss Mercier shortly—the demureness was not lost on her.

Jesanne held her tongue. She had promised her cousin to make the best of things, and she meant to keep her promise if she could. The governess examined the English history, and then laid it aside.

'I don't know this,' she said, 'but I will look through it. Now what is this? Ah, arithmetic!'

She opened it, and her face fell as her eyes encountered the latest methods. 'How far have you gone in this?' she inquired.

'We were doing discount and simple interest,' returned Jesanne.

Miss Mercier turned to the sums, and looked at the methods again. She saw nothing for it but learning them up in her spare time, and the idea did not appeal to her. She put the book down, and took up an algebra. 'And in this?'

'I'm not very far on in algebra,' said Jesanne. 'We were doing simultaneous equations, but I used to get tied up in knots over the problems.'

Miss Mercier's face cleared. 'In that case, I think perhaps you might drop algebra. If you are to have only three hours a day for lessons, we must simplify our timetable as much as possible. Therefore we will leave algebra alone—and geometry too,' she added as she glanced at the next book. 'Now for geography. Let me see this.'

But geography was quite as bad as arithmetic, what with land-tilts, continental shelves, and influence of climate, and so on. Miss Mercier's schooldays belonged to the beginning of the century, before methods were revolutionised, and she knew very little of present-day teaching. She laid the book down in silence, and looked at the French grammar. Thank goodness! This was nothing new—except that it was, naturally, all in French. That did not worry her. The governess both spoke and read French fluently. Jesanne had been taught by the direct method, and, in addition, had had a French girl for a friend since she was a small child. She could chatter easily, and had read a number of French children's books, including most of Jules Verne's romances. Miss Mortimer and her sister, Jesanne's mother, had been educated in a French convent school, and it had been the rule that on three days of the week all conversation was in French. The result was that the girl knew quite a good deal, and Miss Mercier found, with some relief, that her main work here would be to talk and read.

In German, Jesanne was not nearly so advanced, for she had learnt that for only one year, and was not enamoured of it. Miss Mercier, however, decided to continue with it. She hoped by that means to oust the Latin, which, she knew, was well beyond her powers. She set the Latin books aside, and told Jesanne that, for the present, they would concentrate on French and German as being of more use to her when she grew up.

'I believe the Rector or somebody is to take me for Latin,' said Jesanne innocently. 'Didn't Cousin Ambrose tell you?'

'He did not,' said Miss Mercier with a snap. 'I don't see how you are to make time for it, either. However, I will discuss it with him. Now show me your English grammar.'

Jesanne produced it from the pile, and again Miss Mercier found that methods had changed greatly. She realised uneasily that she would have a great deal of private work to do, instead of finding the position an easy one. The truth of the matter was that hitherto she had taught girls who had never been to school, and never went to one until their sixteenth or seventeenth birthdays saw them *en route* for one of the Continental 'finishing' establishments. The standard of work demanded from the average High School girl was a sealed book to her until this moment, and she felt rather appalled as she contemplated the amount of study she herself must put in if she was to teach Jesanne properly.

She meant to do it. If she could keep this post, she would have saved enough from the very handsome salary Sir Ambrose was paying her to give up all work by the time Jesanne was seventeen or so. Then she would take a small house in a good neighbourhood in one of the South Coast watering-places, and settle down to enjoy herself in her own way. But plainly the next three years would be the most strenuous of her career in the way of preparing her lessons.

She looked over the two or three books remaining, and then handed Jesanne the English history and requested her to read aloud. There was no fault to be found here. The girl had been accustomed to reading aloud while her aunt did needlework, and she read clearly and fluently in her well-bred voice. But when it came to dictation, the governess found that the pupil had met her Waterloo. Jesanne's spelling was impressionistic, to put it kindly. In fifteen lines of writing she had twenty-two mistakes. The writing itself was not such as to commend itself to Miss Mercier, being script in the process of becoming running-hand; but it was clear enough, with well-formed letters, and, when it had had time to lose some of its decorative properties and show character, it would be good enough.

By half-past eleven, Miss Mercier had taken a more or less complete inventory of her pupil's acquirements, and knew where she stood. She decided to concentrate for the moment on such subjects as she herself could manage without trouble, and spend the next fortnight in mastering as much as she could of the modern methods in other subjects. She set Jesanne to work with a dictionary to correct her spelling, and by the time Sir Ambrose had come to pay his promised visit, the young lady had three pages filled with neatly written words.

The master of the Dragon House remained only a few moments. He smiled when he saw how his young cousin was employed, and told her to try to notice the shape of words when she was reading.

'That will help you spell correctly far better than writing out words even fifty times each,' he said. 'Don't let her spoil her writing by too much of this, Miss Mercier. I value good handwriting in a woman, and I think Jesanne's promises to be pretty if only she has not to scribble too much while it is forming.'

Then he departed, and, the last word having been written and correctly spelled, Miss Mercier gave history a turn.

But the book was so unlike the ones she had hitherto used. To begin with, it was not divided up into reigns, but into great movements. For example, the whole of one chapter dealt with the Reformation, and covered the reigns of Henry VIII, Edward VI,

Mary I, and Elizabeth. The position of England with regard to the Continent formed the subject of another chapter, and covered the same period. It was very distracting.

And then Jesanne had been taught to think for herself; to reason from cause to effect, and to find out effect from cause. She asked questions, as she had been trained to do in her New Zealand classroom, and they were questions that Miss Mercier, who had never bothered with logical reasoning, found difficult to answer. Finally, she settled the difficulty by forbidding the girl to talk, and telling her to confine herself to answering questions.

Altogether, it was a weary lesson for both governess and pupil, and it would be hard to say which was the more thankful when Agnes tapped at the door to say that Sir Ambrose wished to know if lessons were at an end, and if Miss Jesanne could go to him at once.

'Certainly,' replied Miss Mercier. 'Put your books away, Jesanne, and hurry off. This afternoon we will take a walk, and then you can prepare two pages of this story for French translation, and learn this German verb, and look over the next chapter in your history book. Be quick, and don't keep Sir Ambrose waiting!'

Jesanne scrambled her books together, and shoved them into the shelves anyhow. Then she scampered off, to find that Cousin Ambrose proposed taking her and Miss Mercier for a long motor-run after lunch, as he had to go on business in any case.

'Had a good morning?' he asked her.

'It's too soon to say,' said Jesanne diplomatically.

'Ah? Well, we must wait and see how things pan out. Run along, now, and change, for we must set off immediately after lunch. I'll go and tell Miss Mercier.'

Chapter IX

Christmas is Coming!

The days passed—slowly, on the whole, to Jesanne, who liked her governess no better as time went on. Miss Mercier was a domineering woman, who, as she had said, preferred to have complete charge of her pupils, and had hitherto done so. More than once she hinted to Sir Ambrose that Jesanne should sleep nearer to her, but he refused to listen.

'The Dame's Suite must belong to her—she is the mistress here,' he finally told the governess.

'But she is only a child, Sir Ambrose. Children need watching, and I should really feel much happier about her if I could slip in and see her when I felt it necessary. As it is, there is such a distance between our bedrooms that it is difficult for me to look after her as I should like.'

Sir Ambrose shook his head. 'Child or no, it is our tradition.' Then, as the governess's mouth showed no sign of relaxing, he added, 'Come, Miss Mercier! You, I am sure, must know how tenacious we of ancient stock can be of our traditions. I am sorry I am unable to offer you rooms in the south wing, but there is no space. If your own quarters are not comfortable, you have only to say so and we will do our best to make them so. But I must have Jesanne in her proper place.'

Miss Mercier gave it up after that. She saw that she would never move him from his decision. And she had no wish to change her pleasant abode for any rooms left on that gallery in the south wing. He himself occupied a suite of five; Jesanne's quarters took up four. What were left were two guest-rooms, each with dressing-room and bathroom, and none with a sitting-room.

She left that alone, and concentrated on lessons, which she contrived to make as much as possible like those she had been accustomed to giving.

Jesanne found life hard. She could *not* get out of the practice of asking questions, and trying to go to the root of the matter. When you have been taught to reason out everything, it is very difficult to be content with simply accepting statements.

'If she'd only discuss!' she wailed to her cousin one evening when Miss Mercier had been taken in to Wyesford for a visit to the cinema. 'But when I try, all she says is, "Read what's in your book, and don't ask questions!" That's all very well; but the book never goes far enough. If I don't ask questions, how am I to understand?'

'Save them for me,' said Sir Ambrose soothingly. 'I'll do my best to help you.'

'And she's always saying what a waste of time my Latin is, and wanting me to work at piano. I've got my 'cello, and that's enough!'

'Quite enough!' he agreed. Then he added seriously, 'You see, Jesanne, Miss Mercier is not accustomed to working with a young person from abroad, and I expect she finds it a little strange with such a go-ahead young woman. You must try to be patient. After all, there's only another fortnight of this term left. And I'll tell you something. Next term, I'm giving her the lodge at the west gate to live in. She will have her own maid to look after her, and Spike will see to its cleaning, and so forth. I think she will like it better than being here all the time. I should imagine she would be glad to be rid of you sometimes,' he concluded with a laugh.

'Oh, Cousin Ambrose! What a glorious idea!'

'And then she is so frightened of the dogs. But I cannot

send them out, for even a fortnight of kennels would harm their beautiful manners. But, at the same time, I am sure she really suffers from them.'

'You'd say so if you saw her when Donna and Storm come smelling round her heels,' said Jesanne, laughing. 'Storm was so wicked this afternoon. You know we went for a walk in the park. Well, Carver had them, and Sanchia, and Beowulf out with him. They saw us as we were coming home, and, of course, they came flying to meet us. Even Beowulf galloped for once. She cried out, and Carver called, but they wouldn't go back to him. So I asked if I should go with them, and she said certainly not! I was out with her, and I was to stay with her, and not be so rude.'

Sir Ambrose smiled a little. 'Well; what happened?'

'Well, Carver came up, and he got hold of Beowulf and Donna, but they were as much as he could manage. I put Sanchia on lead, but that bad Storm wouldn't let either of us go near him, and he kept sniffing at Miss Mercier's heels with loud sniffs. His tail was going all the time, and I'm sure he was enjoying himself. But she kept breaking into a little run. And then *he* ran too, and she had to slow down. And she did scold Carver so for not leashing Storm, but how *could* he? Donna wanted to get away, and Beowulf seemed to be infected too. It was all he could do to hold them. And then Sanchia began to prance. It really was awful, and yet it was so funny! I was thankful when we reached the house! And oh! if you could have seen the way she scuttled upstairs to her own rooms! Just like a hen running from a motor.' And Jesanne broke into shrieks of laughter which Sir Ambrose echoed.

'You seem to have had a nice time of it, you monkey! Poor Miss Mercier! No wonder she wanted to get out of the house! I only wonder she doesn't resign her post.' Then a sudden thought struck him. 'Jesanne! You didn't encourage the dogs, I hope?'

'Oh, no, Cousin Ambrose. I don't like her, but I wouldn't do a thing like that. She really looked dreadfully upset.'

'No; I am sure you wouldn't. I must tell Carver to find out where you intend taking your afternoon walk for the future, and to keep the dogs away from the house till you get back. We mustn't torture the poor soul's fears.'

Jesanne looked dubious. Truth to tell, she had thoroughly enjoyed seeing her governess upset. She was a very human girl, and Miss Mercier had been in her most overbearing mood that morning, and had made lessons as trying as possible.

'How long holiday am I to have?' she asked, wisely changing the subject.

'Oh, a month or thereabouts. You break up on the twentieth, and we won't ask Miss Mercier to return till the end of January. And that reminds me, you have had no money from me since you came. Ask her to excuse you at half-past twelve tomorrow, and come to me in the office. I want a business chat with you. Now, what about a game of chess?'

The next morning, as they were sitting down to work, Jesanne duly gave Miss Mercier the message. That lady had got up in captious mood. Reflection on the events of the previous afternoon had shown her that her behaviour had been anything but dignified, and she prided herself on her dignity. So now she raised her brows at the request.

'Why did not Sir Ambrose tell me himself at breakfast?'

'I expect he thought that as he had sent word by me it would be all right,' said Jesanne.

'I prefer to have such instructions direct from himself. Yes; you may go. But please work hard, if you are to lose half an hour of your time.'

She saw to it that her pupil had no chance to do anything but work hard. Arithmetic, geography, French, German, the girl was kept at them with an assiduity that made her long for the end of the morning. She was not even allowed to stop while she had her milk and biscuits which came up at eleven. She had to get through them while writing out the conjugation of a German irregular verb.

But at long last half-past twelve came, and as the clock on the mantelpiece chimed the half-hour, Jesanne asked politely, 'May I go to my cousin now, please, Miss Mercier? It's half-past twelve.'

'Put your books away,' retorted Miss Mercier. 'You must have dictation this afternoon for once. I cannot let you miss it.'

Whatever else was to be said for her, she was certainly making a vast improvement in her pupil's spelling. Dictation every day helped. And when Jesanne found that a spelling mistake in an exercise had to be written out correctly ten times, and saw what inroads this made on her spare time, she got into the habit of keeping her dictionary beside her, and looking up any words of which she was not sure. As her bad spelling was largely the result of carelessness, such methods were bound to meet with success, and already there was improvement.

Jesanne put her books away, and slipped off thankfully to the office, where Sir Ambrose was sitting, looking over some leases that were about to fall due. He raised his head as the child entered, and noted her heavy eyes and flushed cheeks.

'Tired, little maid?' he asked, as he rose with his customary courtesy and set a chair for her.

'Just a little. We've done so much work this morning,' said Jesanne, sitting down with a sigh of relief.

'Well, you must have a good rest this afternoon. What about a gallop with me? I have to go over to Sisley Court about some repairs. Suppose we give Miss Mercier a holiday and have the horses round? Would that refresh you?'

'Oh, ever so much! Thank you, Cousin Ambrose!' And Jesanne looked quite bright again.

'Very well,' he said with a nod.

'Cousin Ambrose—'

'Well?'

'Would you very much mind telling Miss Mercier yourself? I think she prefers that.'

His brows were lowered in a heavy frown as he contemplated the child's anxious face; but all he said was, 'Very well.' Then he sat down at his desk, and picked up a bunch of cheques, riffling through them quickly till he came to the one he wanted.

'Here we are! Now, Jesanne, listen to me. You know that you are my heir. When I die, you will be very wealthy. My mother was an heiress and all her money came to me. Everything will be yours—no; don't speak now. I know what you want to say, and it doesn't really matter. Now, I have seen case after case where a woman who has come into great wealth has either been cheated right and left, or has squandered her money simply because she has had no training. I do not intend that you shall lack training.'

Jesanne looked puzzled. 'How do you mean, Cousin Ambrose?'

'I am going to put you on an allowance. It will be very big for a girl of your age, but I want you to learn as soon as possible how to handle money. I am an old man now, Jesanne. I do not know how long I may be with you—'

'Cousin Ambrose! Please don't talk like that! I hope you'll live another twenty years! *I* don't want any more than I've got!'

He laughed outright at her cry. 'My dear child, please don't wish me anything so awful as to be a centenarian. That's what I shall be if your hope is fulfilled, and I'd rather be excused. However; that's not what we are talking about. I am going to give you £10 a month—£120 a year, that is—and out of it you are to dress yourself, pay for anything you need for your puppy, provide for your amusements—everything.'

'What an awful lot!' gasped Jesanne.

'You will not find it too much, I assure you. Here is an account-book for you. On this side, I want you to write down whatever money you have. On the other, you must put down whatever you spend. And you *must* make your accounts balance. After Christmas, Mr Jennings is going to give you lessons in book-keeping, but for the present this will do. Do you understand?'

'Yes, I think so.'

'I shall look at your accounts each month, and if you can show a balance on the right side, so much the better. You must learn not to be extravagant. At the same time, don't go to the other extreme and turn miserly. *Think* before you spend any money. Ask yourself, "Do I really need this? Ought I to afford it?" If the answer is "Yes," get it. If not, don't. And I need not tell you that you are *never* to run into debt for any reason whatsoever. If you can't afford a thing, no matter how much you may want it, you must go without. And finally, you are not to buy luxuries at the expense of necessities. Now do you understand all that?'

'Oh, yes, thank you,' said Jesanne. 'But it's going to be a dreadful worry. Can't I just go on having pocket-money and you or someone else buy the other things for me?'

He shook his head. 'No; you must be taught to use money rightly, and I think this is the best way. Now, here's your cheque. I've made it a little extra this month, as I gave you nothing last month, and I expect you will want to buy Christmas presents. How much have you in hand?'

'About six shillings, I think,' said Jesanne. 'I bought Auntie Anne's Christmas present and sent it off the last time I was in Wyesford, and it's left me rather bare.'

'I see. But why didn't you ask me?'

'I—I didn't like to,' she answered shyly.

'That's silly! Well, you'll be all right now, won't you?'

'Oh, yes, thank you!'

He watched her curiously. 'You must always be suitably dressed,' he warned her. 'I dislike frills and flounces, especially for schoolgirls; but your clothes must be good. Don't buy shoddy things. It is far dearer in the long run.'

Jesanne knew that already. Auntie Anne had dinned it well into her in New Zealand. How often she had said, 'Buy good, and make it last. It always pays. And *never* economise on gloves, stockings, shoes, or handkerchiefs. And always have your underthings good rather than your frocks and coats and hats if it comes to a choice.'

'I'll be careful,' she promised him. 'And I may choose for myself, mayn't I, Cousin Ambrose?'

'Most certainly you may. If someone else does the choosing, that's not *your* spending the money. And now, I've some news for you that will make you shriek in your favourite parrakeet fashion, I think.'

'Oh, what?' Jesanne looked at him eagerly.

'What do you say to a partner in distress?'

'A partner in distress? Cousin Ambrose, what *do* you mean?'

'Well,' he said, 'Mr Jennings was here this morning, and he tells me that it is all arranged.'

'What is arranged? Oh, Cousin Ambrose! Don't tease so! Do tell me.' For he had stopped tantalisingly short.

'Do you remember that some days ago I told you you might find a new friend?'

Jesanne cast her mind back. 'No; I don't think so.'

'It was the first Sunday Miss Mercier was with us.'

'Ooh! Now I remember! You'd been telling us about Sir Henry Edmunds and how Mr and Mrs Jennings lost little Edris.'

'Yes; that was it. Well, Mr Jennings had already told me that his wife's sister and her husband might have to go out to Burma for two or three years. They have one girl, Lois, who is your age, and Burma does not have the best of climates for a schoolgirl. She is coming to live with the Jennings while her parents are away, and I have arranged that she shall come here and share your lessons and walks and so on. Mr Jennings tells me that she's a very jolly girl, devoted to dogs and fond of games, so I expect you'll get on together all right.'

Jesanne's eyes were sparkling. 'How very jolly! Lois, you say? What a pretty name! We had a Lois at my school in New Zealand—Lois Hardwick. She was one of the prefects, so I didn't have much to do with her, but we all liked her. She was so jolly, and so awfully fair about things.'

'I hope you will like this Lois as well. You ought to, if she is anything like her aunt.'

'Mrs Jennings is a dear,' agreed Jesanne.

'Quite so. Well, now I've finished. Run along and get ready for lunch, and I'll tell Miss Mercier that she is free for the rest of the day, and we'll have our ride this afternoon. Have you any preparation for tonight?'

'German verbs—and an essay on perseverance.'

'Well, you can bring them down to the library after tea and do them there. Now off with you!'

Jesanne shot off to put her cheque safely away, and to ask Agnes to lay out her riding-kit. Then she washed her face and hands, and replaited her hair, and was ready just as the gong sounded for lunch.

Miss Mercier was none too pleased about the turn events had taken, but she had no choice in the matter. Sir Ambrose offered her the use of the car, and told Hiles to take her for a good drive. Then he and Jesanne set off on their ten-mile ride, and when they got back at about five o'clock, the last traces of weariness had vanished from the girl's face, and she was fresh and ready for anything.

Tea was served in the big hall now that the screens were in place. Jesanne loved to sit there by the glowing logs, soft lamplight shedding a mellow glow around, and the pretty tea-table before her. Visitors were very apt to drop in about this time, and she thoroughly enjoyed the importance of pouring out for them and looking after them. Miss Mercier had told Sir Ambrose that she thought it was a pity to bring a mere schoolgirl so much forward, but he had silenced her.

'There is no one but Jesanne to do it—unless I have the servants in, and I do not care for that. Besides, it is good for her to learn to assume these responsibilities. She will have many more and much heavier ones to take over when I am gone. The sooner she learns to act as mistress, the better.'

No one came in that afternoon, and when tea was over, and Miss Mercier had departed to her room, Jesanne went up to the schoolroom to collect her books, and was presently seated at a table in the library struggling with her verb. That done, she turned to the essay. She pulled a long face as she wrote the title. She did so dislike the subjects Miss Mercier set her—'Perseverance,' 'Courage,' and 'A Country Walk in Winter.'

'I wish she'd give me something a little fresher!' she grumbled to herself as she sat biting the end of her pen. "Perseverance"! Ugh! What on earth can I say about *that*?'

And then a sudden idea popped into her head. What had it been but perseverance that had carried Captain Scott and his deathless band of heroes through that bitter struggle back to civilisation which they had only just not reached? What but perseverance that had helped on the pioneers of the British Empire? If they had not owned *that* precious quality, how could they have faced the thousand and one difficulties and dangers they had to meet? Her thoughts went to her own particular bit of the Empire. What terrible dangers the pioneers there had had to meet! The Maori wars—the flooding river, when the work of months might be swept away in fewer hours—the earthquakes and tremors—the appalling eruption of Mount Tarawera which had destroyed the wonders of the Pink and White Terraces, and laid New Zealand for miles around under a thick blanket of ashes, mud, and scoriae—the perpetual hard work for all, man, woman, and child. Had it not been for perseverance, those men and women who had helped to make New Zealand must have failed utterly.

Her thoughts strayed on to another early colony—Canada. What the pioneers there had had to face! The bitter winters when food was practically nil, and they had only log-huts through the chinks of which the fierce polar winds rushed and whistled; the desperate battles with the Red Indian tribes; the fights with bear and wolf and poisonous snake; the awful prairie fires which devoured acres and acres of golden grain just at the moment when it was ripe for the harvest.

Jesanne gave a little chuckle, and settled down to write.

When that essay was handed in next day, Miss Mercier gasped. Her pupil had presented her with six closely written sheets—written on both sides, too—on the subject at the mere sound of which her face had fallen. And it was an interesting essay, packed full of facts. For once the governess was moved from her usual critical attitude, and she congratulated Jesanne on having written something that was really worth reading.

'Now you see what you can do when you try,' she said. 'I hope that, after this, you will always try.'

Chapter X

THE CHRISTMAS SEASON BEGINS

THE remaining fortnight of term dragged by somehow. Jesanne and Miss Mercier struggled together, and, on the whole, it was Miss Mercier who won. After all, she held the trump cards. If Jesanne did not satisfy her, she could always punish her, and she never scrupled to do so. She had made up her mind that the child must be brought under subjection as speedily as possible; otherwise, this sort of thing might continue during the next two or three years, and she found it wearing.

Jesanne was subjected to a sort of petty persecution. Her story-books were locked away if she had not done the amount of preparation her governess deemed necessary. She was sent early to bed for impertinence when she protested. Work was piled on to her so that she found it difficult to fit in her Latin preparation. And when she ventured to tell Miss Mercier that she had thirty lines of Virgil to construe for Mr Farman, the Rector, and so had been unable to finish her other work, she was coldly told that Latin was not to be touched until her general preparation was done.

With this state of affairs going on, it was impossible for the girl to feel either affection or respect for her governess. She was too proud to complain, so formed the habit of waking early and doing her Latin then. Agnes knew about it, and brought her a glass of milk and bread-and-butter at half-past six until Miss Mercier found out one morning, when she peremptorily forbade anything of the kind.

'If you cannot fit in your Latin, I must ask Sir Ambrose to let you give it up,' she told Jesanne. 'You have behaved in a very underhand way about it, and been most deceitful. I knew what would be the result of giving you a bedroom far away from mine! If it occurs again I shall speak to Sir Ambrose.'

'I *must* do my Latin prep,' expostulated Jesanne.

'There is no real necessity. And your health must come first. You are tired out in the mornings before ever you come to me, and your work is disgraceful for a girl of your age. Please let me have no more of it.'

Jesanne was silent, but only with a struggle. However, as working before breakfast was forbidden, she did the only other thing she could do, and prepared her Latin on Saturdays and Sundays when Miss Mercier was free.

On the eighteenth of December, Sir Ambrose sent Totton up to the schoolroom at twelve o'clock, asking Miss Mercier to come to him at once, as he wished to see her before she left for the holidays. Sir Ambrose himself had been suddenly summoned to London, where he would stay for two or three days.

She hurriedly set her pupil a German exercise to do while she was gone, and then descended the stairs, wondering inwardly what Sir Ambrose wished to see her about. He had already sent her the cheque for her salary, with a graceful note saying that he expected she would like to be preparing for her holidays; so it could not be that.

She entered the library to find him waiting for her at his table. A chair had been placed in readiness, and she sat down and prepared to listen.

'I wanted to see you about next term's arrangements, Miss Mercier,' he began.

'Yes, Sir Ambrose?'

'You will have nearly five weeks' holiday. Jesanne is looking tired, I think, and we must not forget that she has crowded a good many new experiences into a very short time lately.'

'I think Jesanne is trying to do too much,' said Miss Mercier, secretly exultant, for this was her chance to put a stop to the Latin.

'Too much? What do you mean?' Sir Ambrose spoke sharply, suddenly anxious. He had thought for the past day or two that his young cousin was not well.

'I think that Latin on top of all her other *necessary* work is proving too much for her. I found that she was getting up at half-past six every morning to do her preparation as she could not fit it in otherwise. I put a stop to it at once, of course. She had been coming to me very tired in the mornings, and her work latterly has been very poor. Once I knew about this early rising to do Latin, I understood it. Seriously, Sir Ambrose, I think it would be wiser to make her drop it altogether.'

He thought the matter over. 'It seems a pity if it must come to that. The Rector tells me she is well advanced, and has been well taught, and she enjoys her lessons. Is there nothing else she could give up instead?'

'I'm afraid not—unless she is to be an ignoramus when she is grown-up. You would not wish her to stop geography or history, I know. Algebra and geometry I have already stopped.'

'What else does she learn?' asked Sir Ambrose curiously.

'The ordinary curriculum. I have given her nothing I have not expected to teach any pupil of mine.'

'Yes; but what are the details?'

Somewhat reluctantly, Miss Mercier gave them, adding, 'You see, there is nothing but what every girl ought to know.'

He considered for a minute or two. Then his brow cleared. 'I have it! She may give up German. She is not very advanced in it, I think?'

'Not yet; but she is making progress. And German is quite a necessary modern language, Sir Ambrose.'

'I never found it so. At any rate, if the child is overworking, something must go, and I would rather it were not Latin. We'll consider that settled, then, Miss Mercier. She will stop German at once. And perhaps it would be as well to set her less preparation.'

Miss Mercier flushed angrily; but she had met her master, and she had the sense to see that it would not do to argue the matter. German must go, and that meant that Jesanne had won in spite of her.

'Very well, Sir Ambrose. It must be as you wish,' she said.

'And you will cut down on the preparation? Indeed, I think she had better have no more this term. She is going to the Rectory this afternoon, and will not be back till bed-time. And tomorrow she has some errands to perform for me. Mr Jennings will come for her. If it is fine, they will ride. If not, they will go by car. I hope to return on the morning of the next day, and as you will be taking the early train to Town, there will, of course, be no lessons. So that's settled. And now I want to speak to you about another matter.'

'Yes, Sir Ambrose?'

'I have seen for some time that our dogs worry you,' he said carefully. 'I have been sorry about it, but I am sure you will see that I could scarcely send them to kennels for the whole of term. That would spell ruin to their house manners. And we have always had house-dogs. At the same time, I am afraid you have not been too comfortable in your rooms. Now I am going to remedy all that. There is a very comfortable cottage at the west gate, and I am having it done up for you to live in. You will be much more private there, and can have your friends—which I hope you are making,' he added courteously, 'whenever you please. A maid will be provided to wait on you, and Spike will attend to the housework. In bad weather, we will send the car across for you, of course, as it is rather a long way away. Indeed, if you wish it, the car will come for you every morning, and take you back after lunch. You will be much more comfortable in your own house, I feel sure, and then you will be free from the dogs.'

Miss Mercier sat literally stunned. This was the last thing she had expected. She knew the cottage he named, for she and Jesanne had passed it more than once during their walks. It was very charming, an old stone erection, with a thatched roof, and a little garden of its own. Jesanne had once brought the keys and showed her the inside. There were four rooms of good size—sitting-room, kitchen, and two bedrooms. A long slip off one of the bedrooms had been converted into a bathroom. In many ways, she would be very much better off. But, on the other hand, it would mean that she would have just so much less control over Jesanne. She did not know what to say, for she knew by a certain tone in Sir Ambrose's voice that his mind was made up, and that if she raised objections she would do herself no good. She said, 'Thank you, Sir Ambrose,' rather flatly, and waited to see if he had any more to say.

But Sir Ambrose had done. He got up, escorted her to the door, and ushered her out. She was thoroughly stunned by the turn events had taken.

The remaining two days went by quietly. Miss Mercier, still under the spell of Sir Ambrose's amazing announcement, treated her pupil quite leniently, and when the morning arrived for the governess's departure for Brighton, where she was to spend the holidays with friends, the child was able to bid her goodbye and a happy Christmas quite sincerely.

Sir Ambrose had not yet returned from London, but Hiles came round with the car at nine sharp, and Miss Mercier was whirled away *en route* for Wyesford and the South Coast, whereupon her unregenerate pupil danced a jig on the top steps, and then, calling to the dogs, rushed off with them to Three Oaks, where she romped violently, coming back at eleven o'clock with a fine colour, and an even finer appetite for her elevenses.

At four o'clock, Hiles came round with the car again, and Jesanne drove to Wyesford to meet her cousin, who was due at five. She did a little Christmas shopping, and then went to the station, where the London train was just coming in. She tore across the platform, and met him with a vociferous welcome.

'Oh, Cousin Ambrose! How nice to see you again! Hiles and the car are outside, and Spike will have tea all ready for us when we get in. Did you have a nice time in London?'

For a moment, Sir Ambrose made no reply. It reminded him too much of the time when three people had rushed to meet him in the same way. Then he saw that his little cousin was looking at him anxiously, so he forced himself to smile and answer.

'Well, little maid? What have you been doing with yourself while I was away? The dogs all right?'

'Fit as fiddles! Is that your case? Have you anything else?'

'No, child. Ah, here comes Hiles. Well, Hiles, all well?'

'Yes, sir.' Hiles took the case and the rug, and held open the door.

'I'll drive,' decided Sir Ambrose. 'Hop in, Jesanne. It's too cold and damp for you to be standing about. What a fog!'

'It's beautifully clear out in the country—or was when we came in,' said Jesanne, hopping into the seat beside the driver.

'Yes—we stand higher than Wyesford,' agreed Sir Ambrose as Hiles shut the door, and then got into the back. 'All right, Hiles?'

They drove off, and were presently through the busy town, and spinning along the quiet country roads, and out of the fog. They made good time, and reached the Dragon House shortly after half-past five. Totton was at the door, and the glow of a great log fire greeted them. So, also, did four excited creatures, who flung themselves first on their master and then on Jesanne.

Tea was ready, and, as Jesanne remarked with much satisfaction, they had the house to themselves.

'I want you to go to bed early tonight, Jesanne,' said Sir Ambrose, taking no notice of this speech. 'You'll be late tomorrow, and later still on Christmas Eve and Christmas Day. You'd better get a good sleep tonight to help you through. Breakfast will be at nine, and I'll be ready to ride with you at ten. After lunch, you've got the decorations to see to, so you've a busy day before you.'

Jesanne agreed unwillingly. She would rather have sat up till her usual time. But he was quite determined, so at nine o'clock she trailed off, followed as usual by Sanchia, and was in bed and asleep by half-past.

The next day was busy. They had their morning ride, and after lunch the men brought in great boughs of holly and fir; trails of ivy; clumps of mistletoe; and armfuls of great glowing chrysanthemums; and, with most of the maids at her disposal, Jesanne spent an agreeable time in turning the hall, drawing-room, dining-room, library, and schoolroom into Christmas bowers. The kitchens were done after tea, and when she finally raced upstairs to change for dinner, she had the satisfactory feeling of having worked hard and successfully, even though her hands were sore with holly scratches.

As for the dogs, old Beowulf had kept gravely aloof, but the three Alsatians had revelled in unlimited opportunities for wickedness. From snatching at boughs and running off with them, to choking over holly and mistletoe berries, they had run the whole gamut, and were now all asleep in the various corners of the library, resting after their labours.

'What comes after dinner, Cousin Ambrose?' asked Jesanne, half-way through the meal.

'The waits,' he told her. 'The Rector's wife is very keen on old customs. Once, I believe, anyone who liked could join in and bellow. But now Mrs Farman trains them, and the singing is really beautiful. Many of the people round here have Welsh blood in their veins—we are on the Marches, you know—and the Welsh have a long tradition for beautiful singing. They come into the hall and sing their carols. Then we have cake and the wassail, and then they sing once more before they go. But they don't come till nine or thereabouts as a rule. They go to the other houses on the way first, and we are the last. It'll be after ten before they leave, I expect—quite late enough for you.'

'We have carol-singing in New Zealand too,' said Jesanne, a wistful look in her dark eyes. 'But it was usually on Christmas Eve.'

'We have a carol service in church then,' explained her cousin as Totton removed the entrée and brought in seasonable mince-pies piping hot from the oven. 'After that, most sensible folk want to get home.'

Jesanne nodded. 'I see. And is that all for Christmas Eve?'

He shook his head. 'No; here we have the Dragon House Ritual.'

She would have inquired further; but her cousin changed the subject firmly, and he did not allow the conversation to return to it.

After dinner, they went to the drawing-room, which was lit up with lamps and a huge fire. Christmas showed no signs of being a white one, but the weather remained damp and raw, and very cold, and the rooms at the Dragon House were large and required much heating. Indeed, Sir Ambrose had been talking lately of having central heating put in—in the downstairs rooms, at least.

But the big excitement for Jesanne was the lighting-up of the great crystal candelabra that hung from the centre of the ceiling. She gave a cry of delight when she saw them, the drops and pendants all glimmering and gleaming in the light of the hundred and fifty wax candles which they bore.

'Oh, Cousin Ambrose! How lovely—how simply perfect!'

'We always light it for the Christmas season,' he explained. 'And, of course, for any great family event. I remember it was lit for my own coming-of-age.' He stopped there. Not even now could he bear to speak of Peter's coming-of-age. Besides, the child had never known Peter, and it might sadden her to no good purpose to be reminded of the cousin whose life had been so tragically cut short.

'Come and sit down, Jesanne,' he said, going over to the hearth. 'That muslin frock you are wearing can't be warm, and this room takes a great deal of heating.'

Jesanne obeyed him, and the dogs all followed. Beowulf sat down at his master's side; but Storm and Donna squatted down one on each side of Jesanne, and Sanchia reached up a pointed nose and laid it in her little mistress's lap. Jesanne sat stroking them all impartially, and gazing into the fire. Perhaps Sir Ambrose's sad thoughts reached her, for she suddenly looked up and said gently, 'Cousin Ambrose, could you—would you—mind telling me about—about Peter—and the girls?'

Sir Ambrose looked at her in silence for a moment. 'Why do you ask that?' he demanded.

'Because—Christmas is the time—for remembering,' said Jesanne unevenly. 'I've been remembering Father all this past week.' Then she added impulsively, stretching out her hand to him, 'Oh, Cousin Ambrose, you don't *know* how I wish it had never happened—how I *wish* Peter were still here!'

Again Sir Ambrose was silent. A memory of Peter's bright face—bright, even that last sad Christmas, when death was coming very near and he knew it—rose up in his mind, and to himself he echoed the child's cry. And yet, as he told himself much later on, he was growing very fond of Jesanne. She could never take the place of Peter and the girls, but she had made her own niche in his heart. Suddenly he spoke, gruffly, because his heart was so sore. 'I'll tell you about Peter and the girls some other time, child. Not now, though.—Ha, dogs! What do you hear?' For all the dogs had suddenly pricked up their ears.

The next moment, Storm and Donna were bounding to the door, baying furiously. Sanchia joined in with puppyish yelps; and even old Beowulf rose and gave tongue to announce the visitors.

'It's the waits!' cried Jesanne, who had rushed to the window and pulled aside the curtains to look out. 'Oh, look, Cousin Ambrose! They're carrying lanterns, just like Christmas cards! And there's someone with a double bass—and some of the men have other things too! And they're singing—what a lovely tune! What is it, please?'

Sir Ambrose smiled as he crossed the room and stood looking out over her head, one hand on her shoulder. 'It's the Gloucestershire Wassail Song,' he said. 'They always sing it up the avenue. It has a swing of its own, I admit.' And above the noise the dogs made, came the lovely, lilting waltz-tune of the Wassail Song. 'They're rather earlier tonight than usual. It's not quite nine. Here; put this thing round you, and come along into the hall to welcome them.'

He tossed Jesanne a great cashmere shawl, smelling of sweet spices and summer odours, and she wrapped it round her shoulders. A stern word brought the dogs to heel, and then they went out into the firelit hall, where the maids were gathering in one corner under Mrs Spike, and Totton was hastening to open the great door, from which the screens had been withdrawn.

It made a pretty picture. The lamplight and fire-glow gleamed on the scarlet and green, white and green, of holly and mistletoe, and on the bronze and golden globes of great chrysanthemums; on the trim black-and-white of the maids and men; on the glossy oak of the walls, and the burnished steel of armour. They touched softly the tall old man with his high-bred face and silver hair, and the slender, dark-haired child in her flowery shawl and muslin frock, and the glistening coats of the four dogs standing round them.

'Patricians, every one of them—master, heiress, and dogs,' whispered the new doctor to his pretty wife as they crossed the threshold. Then both were silent, for the Rector had raised his hand and was speaking his customary greeting at this season: 'Christmas peace and holy mirth be in this house this Christmastide.'

Then everyone pressed in, and Totton shut the door and drew the screens once more. Sir Ambrose, his hand on Jesanne's shoulder, presented her to the little band of twenty-odd who were there.

'Welcome, one and all! This is my heir, Jesanne Gellibrand, who joins me in welcome to you.'

Jesanne felt herself going scarlet, but she held up her head and replied prettily to the friendly welcomes and greetings that reached her on every side. Then the waits disposed themselves in a semicircle; the Rector's wife took the centre; the people who were accompanying—bassoons, flutes, bass-viol, and violins, with one trombone for luck, as the Rector said later—came to the ready. The signal was given, and all broke into the good old carol, 'Good Christian men rejoice!' It was followed by the very old Herefordshire carol, 'Come all you faithful Christian men,' and then they sang 'Stars all brightly beaming.'

Jesanne listened, entranced. For one thing, these carols were new to her. For another, the singing was, as her cousin had said, delightful. And then the setting was so perfect. She declared afterwards that she felt as if she had slipped back a hundred and fifty years or so, and as if she ought to curtsy to anyone who spoke to her!

After the last carol Totton, assisted by his usual coadjutors, and some of the maids, circulated among the company with great slices of the famous Dragon House Christmas cake, which was made from a recipe three hundred years old, and smoking mince-pies. Two of the men came in, carrying carefully between them the great silver punch-bowl which Balthazar Gellibrand had brought with him from Kent, and which was filled with a spicy, steaming mixture whose recipe had come with the bowl. It was set on the table before Sir Ambrose, and he ladled the contents into the tall Bohemian glasses which were ready, and then the maids distributed them, to the waits first, and then to the rest of the party.

When everyone had been served, the Rector stood forward, raising his glass high. 'Long life to Sir Ambrose and Miss Jesanne!' he said. 'May God bless the Dragon House!'

The toast was drunk amid loud cheers which so excited the dogs that they added their share to the noise, and it was some minutes before they could be quieted. Then everyone set to work to dispose of his or her share, Sir Ambrose tasting the wassail, though he refused it to Jesanne with a quick, 'Not unless you want a bad headache tomorrow!' However, he permitted her a slice of the cake, so she contented herself with that, and very good she found it.

When the last goblet had been drained and handed back to old Totton and his helpers, the waits settled down to their final carol, this time singing the exquisite old German carol, 'Silent Night, Holy Night.'

When it was over, there was a hurried tying of scarves and mufflers, a packing of instruments into their green flannel bags, and a lighting of lanterns. Then they made for the door, from which Totton had again removed the screens and which he was holding open. Sir Ambrose stood near it, Jesanne by his side, and shook hands and spoke his Christmas wishes to each one in turn. The

Rector came last, and he got a small packet and a quick, 'For the sick and poor of the parish. May God comfort and shield them this Christmastide!'

Then it was over. The great door was shut and barred, the screens drawn back to their places, and Sir Ambrose, with his hand on Jesanne's shoulder, led the way back to the drawing-room, followed by the dogs. When they got there, the old man sat down in his chair, and drew his little heiress to his side. Jesanne came and stood in the circle of his arm, looking into the heart of the glowing logs. There was silence for a few minutes.

Presently the little girl lifted her head: 'Cousin Ambrose, those words you spoke—were they a—a—?'

'A ritual, do you mean?' he asked. 'Yes; they are said every year when the waits come, and have been said this past three hundred and more years. The chances are that they are even older than that. But that is the first written record we have of them. Come to me in the library tomorrow, and I'll show you the great Journall that has been kept through all the years that the Dragon House has stood—or, at any rate, almost all.'

'*Now*, as well?' asked Jesanne incredulously.

'Yes; even now. And here is another of our traditions for you. It is always written in the same old-world English as when Melchior Gellibrand, eldest son of Balthazar, wrote the first entry in the year 1531.'

'Oh!' Jesanne was awed. 'How—how *very* near that makes it all seem!'

'Yes—very near, after all. Time is but a rolling stream, little Jesanne, as you will find as the years pass. And now,' he added in a different tone, 'are you quite warm? Then I think you had better say good-night and run off to bed. There is more tradition for you to learn tomorrow—very much more. You must be fresh for it.'

'Yes, Cousin Ambrose. And this has been a lovely day,' she

said. Then something in his eyes moved her to lift her face to him as he towered above her. 'Good night, Cousin Ambrose.'

'Good night, my little maid,' he said as he stooped to give her the first kiss that had ever passed between them. 'God bless you, and give you Christmas peace and holy mirth.'

Chapter XI

THE DRAGON HOUSE RITUAL

ALL next day there was, as Jesanne said in her letter to New Zealand later on, a 'waiting' feeling. After breakfast, she and her cousin had a good gallop along the frosty roads. The day had dawned grey and chill, with a silvery rime on everything. But by midday there were pale gleams of sunshine breaking through the clouds, and though the heavy frost still lay, the day brightened.

Cantering quietly homewards up the avenue, Jesanne reined in pretty Rufa just at Three Oaks, and looked round her with a sigh of satisfaction. 'What a glorious day! I was so afraid it would rain, and I didn't want to have my first Christmas in England a wet one.'

Sir Ambrose, who had pulled up beside her, glanced over the landscape. 'Yes; it will be a beautiful first Christmas for you here. We shall not have snow—the glass is too high for that. But the frost should hold. The wind is from the north.'

Jesanne nodded, and set Rufa going at walking-pace. 'The first *cold* Christmas I've ever known.' She glanced ahead as she spoke, and gave a little cry. 'Cousin Ambrose! Look! The house looks like a dragon! It's like a dragon asleep from here!'

He looked in the direction she was pointing, and then down at her with a curious smile. 'So you see it like that?'

'Yes, indeed! But how strange that I've never noticed it before! I've stopped round here dozens of times and looked at it, and I never saw it once. However can that be?'

He laughed. 'There's a legend, Jesanne, that only a true Gellibrand can see the likeness, and he but rarely. Some trick of light and shade, I suppose. For *I* have come up this avenue and paused here thousands of times, I suppose, and yet I have seen the likeness no more than fifty times at most. Still more tradition for you!'

'How very strange!' said Jesanne.

'By the time Christmas is over, you should be soaked in our traditions at this rate. But I have often wondered if you would ever see the likeness.'

'I never did before. But today it's as plain as possible.'

'Ah, well, if proof of your being a true Gellibrand were needed, the old country folk would say we had it now. For it is a fact that none save those of Gellibrand blood ever see it. I have noticed it myself when I have had strangers with me, and they see nothing but an old, sprawling house. Indeed, on one occasion I nearly came to blows with a school friend who was staying with me. He thought I was joking, and bluntly called me a liar. I never tried to get outsiders to see it after that. And yet he was standing where you are now, and looking at it as you are.' He laughed. 'Family heritage is a strange thing, child—very strange. Well, come along. It's cold, for all the sun is shining, and I don't want you to catch a chill. Besides, it must be nearly time for lunch.'

They touched up the horses and cantered up to the house, and as they neared it, the likeness vanished. They took the horses round to the stables, where they themselves unsaddled them, for Sir Ambrose always saw to the well-being of his mount, and had taught Jesanne to do the same.

'Never leave your pony to a groom,' he had told her. 'Always see to her yourself. Then you can be sure that everything has been done properly.'

So the horses were watered, and then turned into loose-boxes to cool off before their riders turned to the house, which they entered by way of the great raftered kitchens, where everything was bustle and hurry. Cook was something of a tyrant; but she was a good-humoured one, and, as Sir Ambrose said, 'If she did chivvy the girls a bit for the good of their souls, it did them no harm, and she was kind enough to them at other times.'

Jesanne raced up the back-stairs to change for lunch, and when she was ready—which was not very quickly, since Sanchia was there and was always more of a hindrance than a help—she went down to the hall by the simple expedient of sliding down the great broad banister-rail. She rolled off at the bottom, and picked herself up to find her cousin watching her from the gallery, and laughing at her tumble.

'Not very dignified!' he told her, as he began to descend the stairs.

Jesanne went red. 'I know. But I have so longed to do it! They are such glorious banisters for sliding.'

Totton emerged from his lair at that moment, to sound the gong for lunch, so no more was said, and in the dining-room Jesanne gradually recovered her normal colour.

After lunch, the dogs had their usual walk, and when they all came in at three o'clock, Sir Ambrose led his young cousin to the library. On the big centre table lay a great tome, bound in black, tooled leather, heavily banded and locked with silver.

With a cry, Jesanne bounded across to it. 'The Journall!' she cried. 'Oh, it *is* the Journall, Cousin Ambrose, isn't it? Oh, open it—do open it! I'm dying to see it!'

He laughed, and produced a silver key with which he unlocked the great book, and then, turning back the cover, pointed to the first sheet.

'YE JOURNALL OF YE HOUSE OF GELLIBRAND,
BEGUN BY
MELCHIOR GELLIBRAND, ESQRE.,

OF YE DRAGGON HOWSE IN HEREFORDSHYRE,
THIS BEYNGE YE TWENTIFIFT DAIE
OF DECEMBRE,
1531.'

she read in big, black-letter script, beautifully illuminated. Even now, after all the years, the colours glowed bravely forth from the yellowed page, little faded from their original hues.

She turned and looked at her cousin. 'How wonderful! Just imagine that lasting all this time! May I read some of it, please?'

He laughed. 'I'm afraid you'll find it rather difficult. Master Melchior Gellibrand wrote a queer, crabbed fist of his own. However, you can try.'

He turned over the page, and Jesanne wrinkled her brows over the straggling, spidery writing with which Master Gellibrand had filled his sheet. After a good deal of difficulty, she managed to make out the first two or three lines.

'Decbr. 25. 1531. This beynge Christmasse Daie, I haue bethought me to write a Journall thatte shalle contayne neues of all thatte doth chance wych shall conserne owre Howse. For wee bee a familie as great as any, and doo holde owre owne wyth ennie in this cowntye.'

'What spelling!' she cried. 'Miss Mercier couldn't talk of *my* spelling if she saw *this*!' She gave Sir Ambrose an impish smile. 'Don't you think, Cousin Ambrose, that bad spelling must run in the family?'

'I never heard that it did,' he retorted. 'But if your very far-away great-grandfather is going to set you such a bad example, I think you had better try another extract. Let me turn it over for you.'

He turned over several great pages, pausing now and then to point out an extract of greater interest than usual. One such told of the casting forth of Nicholas Gellibrand the Parliamentarian. Another was written by Sir Stephen, his brother, and described the bridals of Nicholas and Loveday Penwarne.

'That's where I get that silly name,' said Jesanne pensively. 'Oh, Cousin Ambrose! What's this?'

She had come upon a page headed,

'Ye Draggon Howse Christmas Ritual.'

Sir Ambrose laughed, and turned the pages again, refusing to let her read it. 'Not yet, Jesanne. You shall read it tomorrow if you like. But no heir to the Dragon House ever learns of the Gellibrand Christmas Ritual except from the lips of his immediate predecessor. Throughout the generations there has been only one exception—my great-grandfather, Sir Paul. His parents had been married only ten months when he was born, and his father was killed out hunting before he was a week old. His mother died from the shock, and the boy was brought up by his father's lawyers, and knew nothing of the Ritual until he was a lad of sixteen. Then, one summer holidays—he was at Eton—when he was staying here, he came across the Journall, and began to read, and learned all about this thing. I have never been able to understand why the lawyers had known nothing about it. But so it was. Sir Paul read it over and over again, and thereafter insisted on coming to the Dragon House for Christmas, though before that he had spent his Christmas holidays in London with his guardians. And it has never been allowed to lapse since.'

'But what is it?' queried Jesanne.

'You will learn that later. But I will tell you now that it is very old indeed—far, far older than the Journall, for it goes back to the days when the Gellibrands were lords of lands in Lorraine. They brought the Ritual with them to England, and Balthazar carried it here from Kent. It was left to his grandson, another Balthazar, to write it down.'

'I wonder,' mused Jesanne as he turned the pages for her, 'why Balthazar Gellibrand the First didn't start the Journall himself?'

'For the best of all reasons—he couldn't write.'

'*Cousin Ambrose!*'

'Quite true, little maid. The Renaissance did not reach England till some years after Balthazar's childhood was over, and it wasn't till the days of Henry VIII that Gellibrands were expected, as a matter of course, to learn to read, write, and cipher. They were always a race more given to the sword than the pen. And to this day very few of us have entered the learned professions. We have had sailors, soldiers, even diplomatists, but we can lay claim to very few barristers or parsons. And there is no record of any doctor, though several of our women have been skilled in the uses of herbs and simples, and your great-great-grandmother was noted for her treatment of ailments.'

'I'd rather like to do that sort of thing myself.'

'You must wait till you are a little older. Now look at this. You will find it very interesting. It is an account by Mr Balthazar Gellibrand, who was the father of that Sir Paul I was telling you about, of how he saw the little Princess Victoria—Princess Drina, as she was then called, from her first name, Alexandrina—when she was a baby of two. He gives quite a charming description of her, and speculates as to what will happen if she should ever come to the throne. As you will see, he didn't think it very probable; and doubted very much if it would be good for the country. I'll put in this slip of paper, and we'll read it together tomorrow afternoon if you like.'

'Oh, I should think I *would* like!' cried Jesanne. 'How *very* interesting it all is! Do you know, Cousin Ambrose, next to the lost staircase, I think this is almost the most thrilling thing of all in the Dragon House.'

'Keep a little excitement for other things,' advised her cousin, laughing. 'If you use it all up, I don't know where you will be tonight.'

'Where does it tell about Caspar Gellibrand hiding from the Hanoverian soldiers?' asked Jesanne.

Sir Ambrose turned back the pages, and showed her. 'There it is.'

'Can we read that too, tomorrow?'

'If we have time. But it all depends.'

'Are we to have visitors, then?' asked Jesanne curiously.

'Not that I know of. But other things might intervene, you know.'

'Church, do you mean?'

'Not in the afternoon. And in the evening there will be the Basket to see to. You must help me with that.'

Jesanne sighed rapturously. 'It all sounds too exciting for anything.'

He laid his long-fingered hand of an aristocrat on her head. 'Happy, little maid?'

'Oh yes. Much happier than I ever thought I'd be.'

'But not entirely, eh? What is lacking? I want you to be happy here, child. What more do you want?'

'Oh, well, Miss Mercier is a nuisance, of course,' said Jesanne hurriedly.

He looked at her keenly. 'I don't think you are bothering much about your governess. Besides, she is not here just now, and won't be for some weeks. Come, Jesanne; I wish to know.'

Jesanne turned to him. 'It's only—'

'Well? Only what?'

'Well—I do miss Auntie Anne so.' She spoke in low tones.

'Ah,' he said gravely. 'I was afraid of it.'

She flung her arms round him. 'Cousin Ambrose, I didn't mean to hurt you, but—but you see, she's been like Mother to me all my life. I couldn't *not* miss her, could I?'

He was silent. Then, as she hugged him again, repeating, 'Could I, Cousin Ambrose?' he shook his head. 'No—no; I suppose not,' he said.

What more might have come, there is no knowing, for just then Totton came to announce that tea was ready, so they let the subject drop. But thereafter, if ever he saw Jesanne looking wistful or dreamy, Sir Ambrose was troubled by the thought that the child was missing the aunt who had been mother to her all her life.

After tea she was sent upstairs to dress herself in readiness for the performance of the Ritual.

'What shall I put on?' she asked.

'You will see when you get to your room,' said Sir Ambrose. That was quite enough to send her scuttering up the stairs, followed by Sanchia, who was, however, called back and handed over to Carver, who came to take her and Donna and Storm to kennels.

Jesanne found, lying on her bed, what struck her as a very queer robe of deep blue material, with borders of golden fringe. Mrs Spike was smoothing the folds reverently, and when Agnes came in a minute later to help her little mistress to dress, she gave a gasp, and said in awed tones, 'The Ritual gown! Oh, Miss Jesanne!'

Jesanne would ask no questions of either. Sir Ambrose had said that Gellibrand only learned of the Ritual from Gellibrand. So all she replied was, 'Yes, Agnes. Please help me to get ready.'

Between them, Mrs Spike and Agnes put the robe on her. Then the maid unplaited the pigtails, and brushed the short, thick locks smooth before she bound them round with a fillet of gold. Gold, heelless slippers were put on her feet, and Jesanne stood up, ready. The long loose robe, smelling of half-sweet, half-sharp spices, was too long and wide for her. She saw that the blue was faded in places, and the gold fringe tarnished. Evidently the robe was old, and, just as evidently, of great value. Jesanne felt awed by this very fact, but she lifted her head with the smooth black hair flowing round her small face, and moved slowly to the door.

'Mind and don't step on it, Miss Jesanne,' said Agnes, still speaking in reverent tones. 'You'd best hold it up as you go.'

Jesanne nodded in silence, and left the bedroom and went silently along the corridor on to the gallery, and so down the stairs, her blue-and-gold draperies floating round her and trailing behind.

At the foot of the stairs stood her cousin, clad in a similar robe, but of a rich red. At his side was old Beowulf, and in his hand was an ancient horn lantern, with a candle alight in it. The candle gave out a very feeble spark, and Jesanne wondered at it. However, she said nothing, being overawed by her gown, her cousin's appearance, and the great hush that had crept over the whole house.

Sir Ambrose held out his hand to her. 'Come, Jesanne,' he said; and turned, and led her to the kitchens, followed by Beowulf.

To Jesanne's amazement, the great chambers were empty and in darkness, save for the flickering light of the fire. No one was there; even the two cats had vanished. Her bewilderment was increased when Sir Ambrose, raising his lantern so that the light illuminated faintly every corner of the great place, called, 'Is anyone here? If it be so, then come forth and share our Christmas cheer. For at this season of the year none cometh to the Gellibrands but is fed and comforted in the Name of Christ Who was once denied a resting-place, save among the cattle.'

There was no answer, and presently he lowered his lantern, and led the way to the back kitchen, where the same strange ritual was repeated. Backwards and forwards they went, from one room to another, till even the huge cellars under the house had been visited. Jesanne was awed, almost frightened, and she kept close to Sir Ambrose and Beowulf, who followed them gravely as if he understood what was going on.

They left the kitchens, and returned to the other parts of the house, and again passed from room to room, always with the same challenge in each fresh room; always to find it empty and in darkness, and silent save for the flickering and whispering of such fires as were alight.

It seemed to Jesanne that they must have walked miles. She had never before realised the vastness of the Dragon House, and there was an eeriness about it all that half scared her. Then the beautiful words of the Ritual sounded, and she was comforted. And all the time Beowulf walked with that steady tread, his wise, grave old face intent on what he was seeing and hearing.

At long length they came to the old chapel, and here the words of the Ritual changed. 'Is anyone here? Does anyone seek rest and sanctuary here? If it be so, then come forth and share in safety our Christmas cheer. For at this season of the year none cometh to the Gellibrands but is fed and comforted in the Name of Christ Who was once denied a resting-place, save amongst the cattle, but is now the King of Heaven, throned and crowned with glory.'

As before, there was no answer, only the whistling of the wind through a crack near the window. Sir Ambrose lowered his lantern, and with his free hand on Jesanne's shoulder left the place. Still clad in their falling robes, and with the candle in the lantern guttering to its death, they descended the stairs in grave silence. In the hall, someone had been before them, for over the banister railings hung two cloaks, obviously as old as the robes, and lined and collared with fur. One of these Sir Ambrose threw round the child; the other he donned himself. Another lantern with a fresh candle in it was standing on a little stool close by. It had been lighted, and the tiny flame rose upright bravely. Setting down the first one, in which the candle was flickering out as they passed down the stairs, the master of the house led the way to the great door. He flung it open as far as it would go, and raising the lantern above his head, called in deep, sonorous tones that must have carried far on the clear frosty night the quaint old invitation.

'Is anyone here? If it be so, then come forth and share our Christmas cheer. For at this season of the year none cometh to the Gellibrands but is fed and comforted in the Name of Christ Who was once denied a resting-place, save among the cattle.'

Again there was silence. No one came to respond to the Ritual, and, still guiding the little girl, the master of the Dragon House led the way along the terrace, pausing only at the end to repeat this call. Right round the house they went, and answer there came none. Gazing out over the darkened landscape, Jesanne saw the lights of the village glittering through the leafless branches of the trees, and felt how strange it was that no one should hear that strong, mellow voice calling its invitation in Christ's Name.

At long last they came to the front of the house again, and now she gave an exclamation of surprise. Every window in view was lighted up so that the great, straggling building looked as though it were illuminated in readiness for the Christmas Festival. The door stood open as they had left it, and in the doorway were Spike and Totton to welcome them. The latter took the lantern from Sir Ambrose. Reverently he extinguished the feeble flame before he set it aside, while Mrs Spike hurried Jesanne off upstairs to her own rooms, where Agnes was waiting to help her exchange her archaic attire for a muslin frock.

'Will you have your hair plaited again, Miss Jesanne?' she asked quietly.

Jesanne shook her head. 'No, thank you, Agnes. Just tie a ribbon round my head again.'

That was all that was said. The strange spell still seemed to be hovering over the house, though it was passing slowly away under the influence of the cheerful lights. Sanchia, who had been nowhere to be seen during that awesome pilgrimage, was now curled up in her basket, sleeping the sleep of the justly weary. Downstairs, Donna and Storm could be heard, giving tongue. Slowly the Dragon House was resuming its everyday atmosphere.

But Jesanne could not forget—she thought she never would forget even if she never experienced that Ritual again—the stillness, the eeriness, the beauty of it all. It seemed in some strange way to link her up with people long since dust. But it was not until dinner was over, and she and her cousin were seated in the library, that she ventured to mention it. Then, looking up from the low stool where she sat against his knee, she asked him what it meant.

'It means this, Jesanne,' he said slowly. 'At one time—even just before the last war—there was a legend in the Black Forest that on Christmas Eve Christ walks this earth again as a Man, seeking food and shelter for the night. For that reason, the Black Forest peasant folk always lay an extra place at table. If any knock, they are invited to enter, and share what there is, no matter how little, and lodge the night there, for no man knows whether, in refusing the stranger, he may not be refusing the King of Heaven.

'I suppose that at one time this legend must have been widely spread throughout Europe, and many must have acted on the belief. Among them, certainly, were the people of Lorraine, whence, as I think you know, our ancestors came. At any rate, this was the Ritual prescribed by the Gellibrand family, to be used each Christmas Eve in every nook and cranny of the house, and to be spoken outside the house to all four quarters of the wind, so that Christ, if He should be near, should know that He would be welcome there. And whoever came in reply, even if he were the Gellibrands' worst enemy, was welcomed, fed and housed.

'When the Reformation came, and swept away so much that

was good and lovely, the Gellibrands still kept to the Ritual. As I have told you, we remained Catholic for a very long time indeed, and that, no doubt, helped to preserve it. After that—well, we, as a race, are very tenacious of our traditions. For that reason, whether the idea behind it were believed or not, the Ritual would be upheld. The same thing—or, at least, the same upholding of traditions—happens in many other of the old families. At any rate, as I told you this afternoon, only once in all the years that we can trace back has our Ritual been discontinued—during the early years of young Paul Gellibrand. And you know that as soon as he learned of it, he revived it. What is more, so that it should never lapse again, he framed a decree which is that whoever is in charge of the master of the Dragon House—if that master is only a child, of course—is to read the extract which tells of the Ritual. And the master is to read it for himself as soon as ever he is old enough to understand. Now do you understand, little maid?'

'Yes, thank you,' said Jesanne. She was silent for a few minutes, thinking it over. Then she looked up again. 'Cousin Ambrose, I think it is such a beautiful thing. But why were there only you and me and Beowulf? What had become of everyone else—and the other dogs and the cats, too?'

'It is written and it has always been passed down, that this thing shall be done only by the head of the house, his heir, and one faithful dog, who shall accompany them on their pilgrimage. If, for any reason, the head of the house should be a child, the heir presumptive must go with him. Should both master and heir be children, then the oldest serving-man—and we keep our servants, Jesanne—shall be told of it, and he shall take the children, prompting the master when necessary. And if the master and the heir are babies, then he himself must speak the Ritual. It has always been the custom that as long as the Ritual pilgrimage is taking place the house shall be cleared of human beings and animals. Tonight, the servants were all in the tithe barn; the dogs were at kennels; and the cats were shut into the stables.'

'I see,' said Jesanne. 'Thank you.'

She was very quiet, and Sir Ambrose watched her anxiously, wondering if it had been too much for her.

Suddenly she asked, 'Cousin Ambrose—those robes—and the cloaks—'

'They are part of the Ritual, and must always be worn. They are, I suppose, copies of the attire of gentlemen in the Middle Ages. The present robes are about one hundred and eighty years old. They are always very carefully packed away with certain specified spices and herbs to preserve them. The lanterns are carried in memory of St Joseph, Christ's Foster-father. You know that in most pictures he is portrayed with a lantern? The candles are the old-fashioned rush-lights which we make specially for tonight ourselves. That is why the light is so feeble.'

Jesanne nodded. She was still under the spell of the pilgrimage, and felt disinclined to talk. Sir Ambrose stood up.

'You are tired, little maid. It's been a long day for you, and you will have plenty of new excitement tomorrow. Also, it is after ten. Suppose you run along to bed. Send Agnes down with Sanchia, and I'll take the dogs for their run, and you get off to sleep. I'll bring your baby up to you when I come in.'

'Very well, Cousin Ambrose,' said Jesanne, obediently getting up. 'I'm sorry to be so stupid, but—I can't talk—not just now.'

He nodded. 'I know, child. Run along, and send Sanchia down. Good night, my little maid.'

He pushed back the short, thick hair from her brows, and kissed her, and she went upstairs to send her puppy down to him, and to get undressed and go to bed as quickly as possible.

She was more tired than she thought, and she dropped off to sleep almost at once. When her cousin came in, bringing Sanchia with him, she was slumbering soundly. He put the pup into her basket, bidding her lie down in a low tone that would take no denial. Sanchia was a wise little thing. She curled herself up, and lay with her sharp nose on her bunched-up legs, her bright eyes watching him as he crossed to the bed and bent over the sleeping child.

For a minute or two he stood there, watching her. Then he suddenly bent down and kissed her lightly. 'Good night, little Jesanne,' he said. 'God bless you, for you have given me something to live for, and I am glad indeed that you have come to the Dragon House.'

Then he stole out again, turning the lamp out, and Jesanne slept on, and never knew he had been in, till the pale sunshine of a December morning woke her to the fact that it was Christmas Day; that the bells were ringing merrily from the church tower; and that Sanchia had, in defiance of all rules, jumped on to the bed, and was trying to make a meal of her.

Chapter XII

CHRISTMAS DAY

WHILE she had been undressing the night before, Jesanne had wondered sleepily whether Christmas Day would not seem rather flat after the strange excitement of the Ritual. But now that the Day was here, she forgot about that. She sat up, pushing Sanchia gently to one side and scolding her merrily for coming on to the bed. Then she looked eagerly at the posts at the foot. Big girl as she was, she still hung up her stocking, and she wondered if it had been filled, and if so, who would have done the filling, since dear Auntie Anne was far away at the other side of the world.

Yes; there it was, just as she had tied it last thing the night before, and it was *bulging*! With a whoop of delight, Jesanne scrambled down the bed and unfastened the knot. Then she wriggled back, and with an excited Sanchia to watch, proceeded to turn out the contents.

First came a flat package marked 'For Mistress from Sanchia.' Jesanne bestowed a hug and a kiss on the puppy, and then opened it to find a photo of Sanchia herself in a pretty frame.

'Darling! How ever was it managed?' cried Jesanne.

Sanchia made a playful dart at the stocking, and tried to haul it away, but was stopped in time and put down on the floor, for Jesanne guessed that she would never be able to get on if the wicked pup stayed where she was.

'Cousin Ambrose must have done it while I was at lessons, I suppose,' she said thoughtfully. 'How dear and kind of him!'

Then she turned back to pull out another parcel, just as it had come by registered post from New Zealand. Dear Auntie Anne! Inside it Jesanne found a little red morocco case containing a locket and chain; and when the locket was opened, it showed the copy of a miniature of her own mother and Auntie Anne, taken from one which had been done when they were girls of seventeen and eighteen which Auntie always wore.

'Oh, how darling of her!' murmured Jesanne with happy tears. 'She knew how I always loved that locket. It *is* good of her to send this to me.' She clasped the chain round her neck, resolved always to wear it. The chain was a little long, and would never show under the blouse she wore during the day. In the evenings, she could let it hang outside.

She rubbed the tears away with a corner of the sheet, since her handkerchief was—as usual—missing, and took out the next parcel.

'From Gipsy,' it said simply.

'Gipsy?' Jesanne's laughter pealed through the room. 'What on earth can old Gipsy have sent me?'

It was a pretty dish with 'For Thomas Cat' printed round the rim. Jesanne's eyes widened at this offering. 'But I haven't a cat! Why should Gipsy send me this—unless it's a hint that she'd like to come to the schoolroom and have tea with me sometimes. But I don't think it could be managed. Gipsy does so loathe dogs, and she'd go for Sanchia at once. Why, what's this?' And she picked up a slip of paper which had dropped out of the wrappings.

In an uneducated hand was scrawled, 'Look in the schoolroom Miss Jesanne with love from Cook,' all without any stops.

Like a flash, Jesanne was out of bed and racing across the room to the communicating-door. Sanchia went after her, of course, and Jesanne, with a sudden inkling as to what was meant, sent her back to her basket. Then she slipped through into the schoolroom, considerably startling Agnes, who was busy with the dusting, and gaped at her open-mouthed.

'Merry Christmas, Agnes!' cried the impatient young person. 'Oh, where is it—where is it? I *know* Cook's given me one of Gipsy's kittens!'

With a smile, Agnes pointed out a scarlet-lined basket in the armchair Miss Mercier generally used. Jesanne bent over it, and cried out, 'Oh, Agnes! How sweet of her! Gipsy's prettiest kitten! Oh, *what* a darling! Come to Missus, you sweet!'

'Cook's always said she meant Little Tommy for you, Miss Jesanne,' said Agnes, as Jesanne lifted the fat, sleepily-purring kitten and cuddled it under her chin. 'And the Master says it'll be a good thing for Sanchia, because it'll teach her not to run cats.'

'I must see that she doesn't hurt him,' said Jesanne anxiously. 'She'd never mean to, of course; but he's so little, and she's so big, she might do it when they were playing together.'

'Never you fear, ma'am,' said Agnes. 'Little Tommy has fine sharp claws of his own, and he's well grown, too. He'll teach Sanchia to behave herself, you'll see. But you oughtn't to be here without your dressing-gown and slippers, Miss Jesanne. Shall I fetch them for you?'

Jesanne laughed. 'No, thank you. I haven't finished looking at my other presents yet, so I'll put Little Tommy back in his basket for the present, to finish his nap. Isn't it very late, Agnes?'

'Breakfast won't be till half-past nine this morning, ma'am, as the Master has gone to church. It's just a little after eight, now. You go and see the other things, and I'll bring you some milk,' said Agnes with alacrity.

Jesanne laughed. 'Bring me a piece of bread-and-butter too, will you, Agnes? I was so thrilled last night, I couldn't eat any dinner, and I'm famished now. If I have to wait till half-past nine, I'll expire!'

'I'll bring it, Miss Jesanne,' promised Agnes with a smile. 'You go and get back into your bed, or you'll be catching your death o' cold, and that'll be a nice thing, Christmas Day and all.'

Jesanne went to the door. 'All right. Mind don't let Tommy out, though, or Sanchia might see him and frighten him.'

'I'll see to it. Do go back to bed, ma'am!' protested Agnes.

Jesanne skipped back, and picked up her stocking again. This time she disinterred a well-supplied paint-box, the gift of Miss Mercier, who thought highly of her pupil's artistic abilities. It is regrettable to have to state that the recipient of the gift made a face at the slip accompanying it. Still, it *was* a fine box, with sable brushes, shells of gold and silver paint, and other things not usually in a schoolgirl's paint-box.

'But how on earth whoever filled my stocking put it in, is more than I can understand,' ruminated Jesanne, regarding the long tear she had made in the stocking while extracting the thing.

A packet of chocolate, and an orange and an apple, nuts, almonds and raisins, and a bag of bull's-eyes filled up the foot, with a tiny packet in the toe. Jesanne opened this carefully, and then discovered that she was looking at her first sovereign. A little note said that this was a 'put-off' from her cousin. Her real gift would come after breakfast. In the meantime, he hoped she liked this, which she could have made into either a brooch or a pendant.

'How nice of him! But whatever can the *real* present be?' wondered Jesanne as the door opened and Agnes came in with a glass of creamy milk and a slice of bread-and-butter.

'It's something you'll like, ma'am,' she said as she handed the tray to her young mistress. 'My! I'd have thought I was in fairyland if I'd got a present like that at your age!'

'What *can* it be? Can't you give me just a hint?' pleaded Jesanne.

Agnes shook her head with a smile. 'Oh no, ma'am! What

would the Master say to me? But you'll like it—you'd be a funny girl if you didn't! There; drink your milk, and eat your bread-and-butter, ma'am. I'll go and turn on your bath-water so's to be ready when you've done. It's half-past eight now.'

Jesanne ceased to tease, since she saw that Agnes had no intention of telling her anything. She hurried through her dressing, and when Sir Ambrose came up to the schoolroom, he found her ready and waiting for him.

'Come along, little maid! A happy Christmas to you! Now come down to breakfast, and after breakfast I've something to show you.'

Naturally, after that she was so excited that she could scarcely eat. The dogs were all present, of course, adorned with bows of scarlet ribbon in honour of the day. Sanchia contrived to drag hers off and chewed it to a sodden pulp before anyone caught her; but the elders endured, though old Beowulf kept looking at his master the pathetic question, 'How long have I got to look such a fool, Master?'

But when Sir Ambrose had finished his last piece of toast, Jesanne was to be restrained no longer. Bouncing up from her chair, her short plaits almost standing out at right angles from her head with excitement, she demanded, 'Can't we go and see whatever it is *now*? I'm dying to know!'

Sir Ambrose burst into a hearty roar of laughter. 'You impatient little rascal! Very well, then. Run along and get ready for a walk.'

He was waiting for her when she slid down the banisters five minutes later; and so were the dogs, now deprived of their decorations, much to their relief.

'It's outside, then?' asked Jesanne, as she slipped a hand through his arm.

'It is; and at the south gate,' he replied gravely, a twinkle in his eyes.

'At the south gate? Why, whatever can it be?' Jesanne was completely puzzled.

The south gate to the estate was one that was never used in these days. It was about twenty minutes' walk from the house, masked from it by a clump of tall wych elms. Jesanne had seen it once or twice, but as a rule her activities took her to other parts of the park. She had only passed it in the car during the last fortnight or so, and then she had never noticed it. She knew that it had the dragon gates which all the other entrances had, and that to one side stood a red-brick lodge which, as she had been told, belonged to the days of Queen Anne. The lodge was empty, for, as the gate was never used, there was no need for it. Indeed, the gates were generally chained for that reason. Now, as they turned thither, she was wildly wondering what in the world there could be waiting for her there.

They reached the place, and then she cried out. Why, the lodge was occupied! There were curtains at the windows, and smoke came from two of the chimneys. What could it mean?

She soon knew. Sir Ambrose stopped, and drawing a key from his pocket, held it out to her. 'There, Jesanne! That's my Christmas present to you. The south lodge and all it contains are yours to do as you like with.'

'My very own?' gasped Jesanne. 'Do you really mean it? Oh, but *why*?'

'Because I thought you would like it. It will be somewhere where no one has any right to follow you without your permission. Of course, I expect you to use it in reason, and not to abuse the privilege,' he added. 'But here you will be quite private, and I intend to let the household know that it is my wish. Jennings tells me that his wife's niece will be here at the end of the week. I expect she will be a nice friend for you, and you can invite her here, and no one will interfere with you. There is only one condition. You are to keep it in order yourself. *You* must see to the sweeping and dusting. If you want to cook, there is a capital little oven in the kitchen, and you can make what messes you like, provided that you clear up after you have finished. One of the kitchen-maids will see to the very dirty work, such as the cleaning of the stoves, for you. The rest you must do for yourself. Now, suppose you use that key and let us into your domain.'

Jesanne was so excited that she could scarcely get the key into the lock. It was done at last, and they entered. The door opened into a tiny hall, with three pegs for hats and coats. From one side opened the kitchen, where they went first. It was a charming little place, with its walls freshly papered with a floral paper. A small table stood by the window, and three windsor chairs were set against the walls. Opposite the window was an old Welsh tri-darn, with quaint old 'dragon' china on it. An eight-day clock hung on the wall, solemnly ticking out the time. On the mantelpiece were two china dogs, two brass candlesticks, and a small brass preserving-pan, all as bright as hands could make them.

Sir Ambrose opened the doors of the tri-darn, and showed piles of dusters and kitchen towels, and in the lower half of the closet by the side of the fire were all kinds of polishes and brushes. The upper half held a pretty, old-fashioned, floral tea-set. The closet at the other side held stores of various kinds.

'You can get milk and butter and so on as you want them from Spike,' said Sir Ambrose. 'Now come and see the rest.'

He led the way into a dainty parlour; where the crowning glory was a sewing-machine. It was a hand machine, and far from new, but Jesanne gloated over it. It had been put into good order, and she saw herself getting through various kinds of mending at express speed, and with very little trouble. Sewing was no favourite of hers, and mending she abominated.

Upstairs were two dainty bedrooms, and over the little hall a tiny bathroom had been made. It was all very complete, and an ideal 'play-house' for any girl. Jesanne took in all the richness with flushing cheeks and eyes growing more and more saucerlike.

'It—it's simply *wonderful*!' she cried at length. 'Fit for a queen. Why, Auntie Anne could live here!'

Sir Ambrose flushed darkly. 'I hope,' he said a little stiffly, 'that if Miss Anne Mortimer should ever come to pay us a visit, she will come to the Dragon House. I should not dream of permitting her to use a mere cottage like this.'

'*What?*' cried Jesanne in startled tones.

'If your aunt should ever come to pay us a visit, I trust she will accept the hospitality of the Dragon House. Now tell me, do you like this?'

'I'd be lacking if I didn't,' said Jesanne simply.

'Then I am very glad I thought of it. I think that every girl should be taught the rudiments of housework, arid it seemed to me that to perform these duties in your own little house would be much pleasanter for you than to perform them in your own rooms. Remember, it *is* to be kept in proper order. I shall expect you to invite me to have tea with you,' he added, laughing, 'and I shall also call on you. If it is not as it should be, how ashamed we should both feel!'

'I'll keep it like a new pin,' promised Jesanne. Then she stopped.

'Cousin Ambrose, how am I to manage when lessons begin again?'

'You will always have your afternoons,' he said. 'Miss Mercier will lunch with us; but after that she will return to her own lodge, and you will be more or less your own mistress from, say, half-past two onwards.'

The chiming of the wall-clock roused them both to a sudden

sense of the time. 'Half-past ten!' exclaimed Sir Ambrose. 'Come along, or we shall be late for church.'

He hurried her off, and by dint of speeding they reached church in time for the eleven o'clock service. After that, and a few minutes in the churchyard, spent in greeting everyone, they returned to the Dragon House, where dinner—there would be only supper tonight—waited for them. But after dinner, and an hour or so spent on the Journall, Jesanne went off to seek Mrs Spike and beg various stores she wanted, and then she raced away to the south lodge, accompanied by all the dogs. Her cousin had agreed to have tea with her this afternoon, and she wanted to have everything ready for him when he walked across at four o'clock.

Chapter XIII

A Christmas Surprise

JESANNE was very busy in her little kitchen when she heard steps on the brick pathway outside, and then a knock at the door. She ran to open it, followed by the three Alsatians, though old Beowulf merely lifted his head as he lay in a warm corner by the fire, and then laid it down again. To her unbounded surprise, she saw not only her cousin, whom she had expected, but a tall, pretty girl with a very woebegone face.

'Ah, Jesanne,' said Sir Ambrose as he laid a kindly hand on the arm of the newcomer. 'Here's a surprise for you! This is Lois Bennett. She came earlier than was expected. Mrs Jennings rang me up shortly after you left to say that her niece had arrived, and to ask if you might go to tea with her. However, I told her what was happening, and suggested that Lois should come here instead.'

'Oh, what fun!' cried Jesanne. 'Come in, both of you! Cousin Ambrose, you go into the parlour while I take Lois upstairs to take her things off.'

He nodded. 'Thank you. May I smoke?'

'Yes, of course! Do whatever you like. Come along, Lois. We'll go upstairs for you to take your things off, and then I'll show you the whole house.'

Sir Ambrose laughed as he hung up his cap and coat, and then sauntered into the parlour, calling the dogs with him, while Jesanne escorted her visitor upstairs to the pretty bedroom with its paper of twining briar roses, its little white bed, and the graceful Chippendale furniture, which, as Sir Ambrose had told its new owner, had all come from the Dragon House. Indeed, as Jesanne told Lois later on, beyond the dusters and other household appliances, there was very little that was new, everything having come from the Dragon House, which could have spared furnishings for two more baby-houses of this description and never missed it. So the gift was not quite as extravagant as it seemed at first.

But this came later. Now, Jesanne, inwardly a little shy, led Lois to the bedroom, and sat on the end of the bed, watching her as she removed hat and coat.

'How tall she is!' she ruminated. 'She must be sixteen, at least! And isn't she pretty—if only she didn't look so miserable! I wonder what's wrong with her?'

As if she had spoken the thought aloud, Lois turned to her and said simply, 'It is good of you and Sir Ambrose to ask me—and on Christmas Day, too!'

Jesanne pulled her down on to the bed and took hold of one hand. 'But it's lovely of you to have come! It was dear of Cousin Ambrose to bring you. It's marvellous here, but it does get lonely sometimes—especially when you've been accustomed to being with lots of other girls all the time. Being only one takes some getting used to!' With which appallingly ungrammatical remark she stopped, apprehensively, for Lois turned her head away, and blinked fiercely.

'What's wrong, old thing?' pleaded Jesanne. 'Oh, I say! Don't cry—please don't cry!'

For Lois had suddenly stretched her arm along the bed-rail and laid her face on it, and her shoulders were shaking.

'It's just—they've had to go early—Mummy and Dad,' she choked. 'Dad got the cable yesterday—had to go at once—c-could, because anyhow we'd shut up the house—were in digs. And so—and so—'

'And so they could go at once,' Jesanne finished for her. 'Oh, *don't* cry, Lois! They'll come back to you, you know.'

'What difference does that make *now*?' sobbed Lois.

'Only—that they *will* come back.' Jesanne had to exercise great self-control to keep her voice from shaking. 'When you—know—they won't—it's different.'

Lois gulped. Then she lifted her head and looked at her companion. 'You mean—you mean—oh, yes; I know. I'm sorry, Jesanne. I'm a selfish pig to upset you like this! And on Christmas Day, too! Only—it did seem so dreadful. And we've never been apart for Christmas before.'

'Here's a hanky,' said Jesanne, pressing her own into the hot hand she had been holding. 'Don't cry, Lois. It's only for a time, and then they'll come back to you.'

Lois mopped her eyes, blew her nose, and then sat up. 'Thank you, Jesanne. It's awfully decent of you. I'll try not to be a baby again, truly I will.' She gulped, showing that her recovered self-control was none too steady yet, and Jesanne, with a wisdom born of her own experience, hastened to change the subject.

'Look at the bedroom, Lois. Isn't it pretty? And I've been asking Cousin Ambrose, and he says there's no reason why we shouldn't sometimes spend a night here, so long as we have the dogs with us, and Agnes—she's the schoolroom maid—to be someone grown-up. Won't it be fun? There's a camp-bed in the cupboard, and heaps of room for it to stand under that window.'

Lois stood up, giving her eyes a last violent scrub. 'It's tophole, Jesanne. What a gorgeous present!'

Jesanne nodded importantly. 'And the best of it is that no one can come in unless I invite them—that means that Miss Mercier won't come. Oh, Lois, she's an utter horror! She thinks I ought to sleep in her room, so as to be always under her eye! And she hates dogs, and is *terrified* of Alsatians. It's so trying, because

I have my pup, Sanchia, and then there are Donna and Storm, Cousin Ambrose's Alsatians.'

'Oh, how can she?' cried Lois. 'Why, I love Alsatians— they're so wise, and so loving and faithful!'

'Well, she does, anyway. But never mind her! She won't come back for a month, anyhow. And I do want your help so.'

'My help? What for? I mean, how can I help you?'

'I'm going to look for the Lost Staircase'—Jesanne always spoke of it as if it had capital letters—'and two will be better than one for hunting.'

Lois gasped, as well she might. 'But I don't understand in the least! *What* lost staircase? How could a staircase be lost, anyhow? it's much too big! Are you pulling my leg?'

'Oh, no!' Jesanne assured her earnestly. 'I'll tell you all about it later. Meanwhile, there's Cousin Ambrose yelling for his tea, so we'd better go down and see about it. Men,' added the experienced Jesanne wisely, 'are so impatient!'

They peeped into the other bedroom and the bathroom; and then, as Sir Ambrose's calls were growing importunate, raced off downstairs, to find him standing in the middle of the kitchen, looking rather helpless, and holding in his hands a tray of nicely browned light-cakes.

'Come along, you two!' he said. 'What have you been doing? Jesanne, these things were beginning to burn, so I took them out. Where shall I put them?'

'My light-cakes!' shrieked Jesanne. 'Oh, are they badly burnt?'

'No; just one or two. Where do you want them put?'

'On to this plate.' She took it from the rack above the fire. 'It's all hot and ready. Lois, the butter's in that cupboard if you like to butter them while I make tea.'

Lois got the butter, and found a knife, and Jesanne made the tea in the old silver teapot. The table she had set already, with the pretty blossom china which, so Sir Ambrose told them, had been a wedding-gift to his mother ninety years ago. 'I gave Jesanne that instead of buying anything new,' he explained to Lois when she exclaimed with delight over its daintiness. 'I've noticed that she seems to prefer old things.'

'So I do,' said Jesanne as she handed the cups. 'I think these are simply lovely. You couldn't buy anything prettier if you tried with both hands! Have a light-cake, Lois. Luckily, they aren't all burnt.'

Tea was, after all, a light meal. Sir Ambrose had to taste his young cousin's baking, and pronounced the light-cakes very good. But after the substantial midday dinner no one really wanted much of anything. Mercifully, Jesanne's cakes were small, and she had cut the rich fruit-cake, which had been Mrs Spike's offering, in wafer slices. Sir Ambrose took advantage of the fact that the dogs were present, and while the two girls chattered excitedly about the cottage, the four had a surprise meal. However, the plates were cleared, and the cook's feelings not hurt, which was the main thing. Then the girls washed up, and put the china away, and after that, Sir Ambrose called them to come home.

'If you mean to help with the Basket, it's time we were making tracks,' he told them. 'Cover your kitchen stove, Jesanne. The fire will soon be out. And there's a guard somewhere for this one. Then you can be sure it's all safe. Now run along and get your hats and coats. I'll put out the lamps and turn the dogs loose.'

The pair went off upstairs, and when they came down again, Jesanne's little domain was in darkness, except for the light from Sir Ambrose's electric torch which he held up to show them the way. Then there was the thrill of locking the door behind them after a final look-round to be sure that all was safe. That done, they turned and walked homewards through the park, the dogs gyrating madly about them.

When Mr Jennings had brought Lois over to the Dragon House that afternoon, he had, by special request, also brought a small case containing her white frock and other things, ready for the evening. Sir Ambrose would have gladly kept her all night for Jesanne's sake, but he knew that Mrs Jennings would want to see something of her niece, so he forbore to give the invitation. There would be plenty of time for that later.

'What a height the child is!' he thought as he walked to the Dragon House between the two girls. 'She must be two or three inches taller than Jesanne, and she's only a month or two older.'

It was the more surprising in that the Gellibrands were a tall race; but Jesanne was like her mother there.

'What did Sir Ambrose mean about "the Basket"?' asked Lois curiously of her new friend as they changed in Jesanne's room, with Agnes hovering round to see that everything was right.

Jesanne shook her head. 'I've no idea. Agnes—'

'I can't tell you, Miss Jesanne. The Master wouldn't like it,' returned Agnes primly.

'Oh, well, we'll soon know now,' said Lois. 'In the meantime, you tell me what you meant by the lost staircase.'

'Too long to tell,' decided Jesanne. 'Wait till later—tomorrow, perhaps.'

'Oh, you *are* aggravating!—Bother my hair!' Lois was combing out the thick mat of curls that rioted over her head, and was finding it a painful process.

'I love your hair,' said Jesanne. 'I've got to let mine grow. I began just before Daddy—died. Then Auntie Anne said I'd better go on, and as it's long enough to plait now, it would be stupid to cut it at present, anyhow.'

'I've got to let mine grow too,' said Lois, as she made a careful parting. 'Daddy and Mummy expect to see me with it tied back when they—come back.'

'Well, it ought to look very nice—it's so pretty and curly! Mine's as straight as a barge-pole,' said Jesanne mournfully.

'Yes; but it suits you, you know,' said Lois with a glance at the silky masses of waveless black hair that were caught back from Jesanne's clear-cut little face with big white bows, to fall just below her shoulders. 'And having curly hair isn't all jam, you know. When you've been out in the wind, it hurts horribly to comb it out.'

'I hadn't thought of that,' admitted Jesanne. 'There! I'm ready at last! Are you done, Lois?'

'Just my frock to put on.' Lois laid the brush down, and looked for her frock, which Agnes was holding in readiness.

It was slipped on, and the maid twitched it into place with deft touches. Then she stood back to be sure that nothing was lacking.

'I think that will do, Miss Lois,' she said at length. 'Here's your clean hanky, Miss Jesanne. Miss Lois, have you yours?'

Lois produced it, so Agnes let them go.

'What a fuss!' observed Lois as they walked down the corridor.

'Cousin Ambrose is particular,' explained Jesanne. 'He doesn't *say* anything, but he *looks* a lot.'

'That's worse. Oh, Jesanne! What lovely carving!' She came to a dead stop before one of the panels, looking at it with eager eyes.

'Yes; isn't it?' said Jesanne. 'This is the Angel Gallery. Upstairs there's the Hunters' Gallery. It's all carved with hunting scenes. I'll show you tomorrow in daylight.'

'You have a lovely home.'

'It's not bad,' agreed Jesanne. 'Come on! We'll be late if we don't hurry, and you'll have heaps of time for looking at it all later on.'

She flung a leg over the banisters, and slid down at top speed. Lois looked, and then followed her example, shooting down with such velocity that the pair crashed, and rolled together at the bottom, where Sir Ambrose had to pick them up.

'Nice ladylike behaviour!' he said with mock severity when he had assured himself that no one was any the worse.

'But it's such a lovely feeling—almost like flying,' said Jesanne.

'It's as well Miss Mercier isn't here. I don't think she would easily recover from the shock of seeing that performance. Well, if you two don't want to perform any more acrobatics, suppose we go in to supper.'

Supper was more or less of a farce so far as the two girls were concerned. They were both so wildly curious about 'the Basket' that they shook their heads even at one of Cook's best trifles. And Sir Ambrose was no help. He not only refused to answer any of their questions but even teased them by prolonging his own meal. However, he finished at long length, and then he rose, telling Totton to leave the table as it was for the present.

'I expect the young ladies will be glad to come back to Cook's trifle when all the excitement is over,' he said, laughing.

Totton smiled sympathetically. 'Yes, sir,' was all he said, however.

Sir Ambrose took an arm of each, and ran them before him through the great hall and into the drawing-room, where Lois exclaimed over the beauty of the four great candelabra, which were all filled with lighted wax candles.

'I've seen chandeliers like that in show houses,' she said, 'and I've often thought how lovely they must look when they're all lit up. But I never thought I'd *see* one.'

'And look at our decorations!' cried Jesanne. 'If you'd been here yesterday, you could have helped—Oh! What's that?'

The two girls danced across the room to a great refectory table which usually stood at the back of the hall, but which was now set against the far wall, with tableaux of the Christmas story arranged on it. There was one of the angel speaking to the shepherds, with tiny sheep and lambs lying about them. Another showed St Joseph and the Blessed Virgin at the door of the inn; a third was of the stable, with delicately made angels clustered all around, and the oxen, the asses, and more sheep mingled with them; a fourth was a representation of the worship of the shepherds. The little figures were all beautiful, and, as Jesanne instinctively knew, all old.

'Another tradition, Cousin Ambrose?' she asked, smiling up at him.

He nodded. 'Yes; this has been done for many centuries so that the children of the house should really see what the First Christmas was like—as far as we can imagine it,' he added. 'The figures date back to the days of James II, and come from Dresden. Before that they were made of wood. Unfortunately there was a small fire here then, and they were all burnt. The Gellibrand of the period sent to Germany for these to take their place. There is still the visit of the Magi to add, but that is never set out till the eve of the Epiphany. Now we'll have the Basket. The servants will all be here in a moment.'

The two girls followed him across the room to where a tall Chinese screen had been set across one corner. He moved it aside, leaning it against the wall, and there stood an enormously tall hamper, nearly up to Jesanne's shoulder. Large parcels were heaped on the floor round it, and above it shone a Della Robbia plaque with a beautiful Bambino on it. Jesanne looked up at it, quick to feel the symbolism.

'The First Christmas Gift,' nodded Sir Ambrose, following her gaze. 'Ah! Here come the household! Now we can get to work!'

They came trooping in, headed by Spike and Totton, to form a half-circle round the hamper. Jesanne saw that not only the house-servants but the men who worked on the estate were present. When they were all in place, her cousin raised his hand, and at once they all sang, without any accompaniment, the beautiful old 'Adeste Fideles.' Then he read St Luke's account of the First Christmas, and followed with the usual evening prayers. When they had risen from their knees, he spoke a very short address, telling them all that he hoped they would like the gifts waiting for them in the Basket, but that they would not fail to remember the great Gift of Christ Whose Birth they were commemorating. Then he called on Jesanne and Lois to begin to distribute the gifts, Agnes having brought a stool for her little mistress that she might reach more comfortably.

The Basket was piled high with parcels of all shapes and sizes, and Jesanne and Lois found that their work was to take one each, and hand it to Sir Ambrose, who called out the names, when the recipients came to get them.

The first two were for Gladys Owen and Silas Hiles, and one of the housemaids and the head-gardener came up to receive them. The next two were for Totton and Agnes, and as the maid went away smiling, Jesanne, who had recognised her own parcel of handkerchiefs, hoped anxiously that she would like them.

Much to their amazement, Jesanne and Lois came next. Then Sir Ambrose and one of the cowmen were called. And so the fun went on, the Basket becoming beautifully empty, and Jesanne more than once nearly pitching head first into it as she stretched down to get another package. The piles by everyone were heaping up, and all remained unopened, for, as Sir Ambrose explained, it was not considered good form to open anything until everyone had been served.

When the Basket had been emptied—which was not for some time—the bundles at the sides had to be tackled, and, with shrieks of laughter, Jesanne produced a thick one for Beowulf, while Lois's choice was a small flat affair for Gipsy, the handsome Persian cat who ruled the roost in the kitchen. Beowulf came to receive his own; but Cook undertook to deliver Gipsy's, that haughty being refusing to tolerate any dog that ever walked. There were large parcels for Donna and Storm, and a smaller one for Sanchia, and quite a little one for Little Tommy, who was enjoying the whole width of the schoolroom hearth to himself. At length, everything had been delivered, and then two of the men removed the Basket, and everyone—with the exception of the dogs, who were *not* encouraged—began to open their gifts.

Jesanne rejoiced over a pretty string of amber beads from her cousin, even while she voiced her surprise.

'You gave me so much this morning, Cousin Ambrose, I never expected anything more,' she said.

As a matter of fact, she had quite a little pile to examine, for everyone in the household had remembered her. Mrs Spike had contributed a hot-water bottle with a fine knitted cover; Agnes had made a very dainty handkerchief sachet; Carver presented a new scarlet leash for Sanchia. Besides these, there were handkerchiefs, chocolates, and piles of other oddments from the other servants, who were all rejoicing in the handsome presents that the master and his heir had given them. As for Lois, she found a string of lapis-lazuli which just matched her eyes, from Sir Ambrose; a napkin-ring of carved olive-wood from the dogs; a silken eastern shawl from Jesanne; and a beautiful little carved ivory model of the Taj Mahal from the cats.

All of this was so thrilling that she had no time for fretting, and when Mr Jennings arrived at ten o'clock to take her home, instead of the Niobe he had dreaded finding, there was a very tired but smiling girl, who said she had had a really splendid time after all. Lois was so weary that when she did get to bed, instead of crying herself to sleep, as she had fully intended earlier in the day, she just curled up, and was 'off' as soon as her head touched the pillow.

'Has it been a happy Christmas, little maid?' asked Sir Ambrose as he and Jesanne sat by the dying logs in the drawing-room, waiting for the dogs, whom Carver had taken for their last-minute run.

'Very happy, thank you,' said Jesanne.

He looked at her. 'I know what you want still,' he said. 'Jesanne, don't be impatient, child. There's no knowing what next Christmas may bring forth. Now, we won't talk of it. I've got a lot of pride to swallow, and no Gellibrand of us all ever likes eating humble pie. So hold your horses, and say nothing. Here comes Carver, so you'll be able to retrieve your baby and get off to bed before you *quite* take in the whole place in one of those enormous yawns.'

Jesanne laughed shamefacedly. 'I'm sorry to be so rude, but I am *so* sleepy.'

He laughed. 'It's been a long day, and packed with thrills, I know. I have told Agnes not to wake you in the morning, for you've had an exciting two or three days. Now be off to bed with you! Got all your parcels? Good night, then, little maid. Sleep well; and God bless you!'

'Good night, Cousin Ambrose,' said Jesanne sleepily. She kissed him, suppressing a cavernous yawn to do so, and then trailed off upstairs so drowsily that Agnes had very nearly to undress her and put her to bed like a baby. Sanchia was already installed in her basket, apparently as completely sleepy as her little mistress.

Agnes tucked the child in, turned out the lamp and lit the night-light which was always burned so that if Jesanne had to get up to take the puppy out there was light for her. Then off she went to her own room, quite unaware that as soon as her back was safely turned, a wicked black-and-gold puppy would leave her own bed, leap up beside her mistress, and spend the night curled down at her back in complete happiness.

Chapter XIV

The Lost Staircase

NEEDLESS to state, the best part of the next day was spent in the south lodge. Mrs Jennings had a sudden summons to Ludlow, where her mother lived, and Lois was driven up to the Dragon House quite early, and left there for the day. The weather was cold and damp, with a thin mist straggling eerily across the landscape. Sir Ambrose saw that both girls were well wrapped up, and then took them for a sharp walk with the dogs. But by noon they were in Jesanne's baby-house, where Agnes had already lit the fires in the kitchen and sitting-room, and were preparing lunch for themselves, Mrs Spike having sent a basket across with the maid, who stayed there to look after them.

The three Alsatians also stayed, though Beowulf followed his master when that gentleman returned to the house, intent on business of his own.

'I'll walk down for tea,' he promised Jesanne, who had clamoured for his company. 'But I may have a caller or two, so I can't stay now. Don't set yourselves on fire; don't poison yourselves; don't give the dogs any potato—it's poison to Alsatians, and not fit for dogs in any case. Goodbye!' And he marched off.

When he had gone, the girls set to work to peel potatoes, prepare sprouts, and make custard sauce for the tiny Christmas pudding they had found in the basket. They did it all themselves; Agnes was bidden find a chair and leave them to it. All the same, she kept an eye on them, and gave them sundry useful hints.

Lunch over, she insisted on washing-up, and then departed, as she was to have the half-day's holiday. They had the dogs, and Sir Ambrose would be down by four o'clock, so it was unlikely that they could come to much harm.

When she had gone, and they were curled up on the little couch by the fire, sucking oranges, with the three dogs sprawled on the rug beside them, Lois turned on Jesanne, and demanded an explanation of her mysterious speech about the lost staircase.

'I simply don't *see* how a staircase could be lost,' she said. 'Explain, please!'

Jesanne threw the orange-skin into the fire, wiped her fingers on a handkerchief that had seen better days, and settled herself more comfortably. Then she began. She told the story as vividly as she could, and Lois became as excited over it as the most exigent could have wished.

'And no one's ever found out where it went? Jesanne—what a *thrill*!'

'Of course they've tried,' said Jesanne, who was gazing dreamily into the fire. 'But no one has any idea where it could have been. All anyone seems to know is that it *was* there; and then it went. It certainly can't have been anywhere about the Angel Gallery. As Cousin Ambrose says, they would never have covered up such marvellous carving, and you can see for yourself that none of it was put in later on.'

'I don't see that. It *might* have been. Of course, it's very wonderful, but they could have had it copied,' said Lois.

'That's what I thought; but Cousin Ambrose says they've had some of the cleverest ark—ark—you know; those people who know all about ancient things—to see it, and they say that the carving was all done by one man. *I* don't know how they know. But that's what they say.'

'And it couldn't have been where they broke in the wall to make the corridors? It's an utter mystery!'

'Oh, no; Cousin Ambrose says there wouldn't have been room.'

'Then where on earth could it have been? How do you think we'd better start looking for it?'

'Well,' said Jesanne slowly, 'I thought we'd better read very carefully through that part of the Journall that tells about the time when it must have been taken down.'

'But you said that Sir Ambrose says that it says nothing about it,' objected Lois.

'I know. But we might get some sort of hint.'

'Oh, well, I'm game for anything. Can we have the Journall down here, do you think?'

'Of course not! Cousin Ambrose would never allow it! We'll have to read it in the library at home. But that needn't worry us. There are bits that are quite private, but they don't come in the part *we* want. The worst will be trying to make out the writing—*and* the spelling!' Jesanne paused to giggle. 'I'm going to ask Cousin Ambrose if I can show some of it to Miss Mercier. Then, perhaps, she won't have quite so much to say about *my* spelling!'

'Is it so awful?'

'Whose—mine, do you mean? It's not brilliant.'

'No, no! The people's who wrote the Journall!'

'It's ghastly. You wait till you see it.'

'When will that be?' Lois was not patient by nature, and she was quite as excited over the staircase and the Journall as even Jesanne had been.

'After tea, I expect. Anyhow, I thought we'd ask Cousin Ambrose if we could change for dinner then, and spend the time from then till dinner hunting through.'

'Oh, good! There wouldn't be any time *after* dinner; that's certain. Auntie will be coming home, and they're to call for me on the way.'

'And Cousin Ambrose said I must go to bed at nine tonight because I've been having such late nights lately. What time is it now, by the way? Half-past three? Then if we're going to make scones for tea, we'd better begin.'

They made their scones, and when Sir Ambrose arrived at the little house at a quarter-past four, he found tea ready for him in the pretty parlour that was gay with evergreens, lamplight, and firelight. When the two girls put their request to him, he consented with a laugh.

'So you want to try to solve our family mystery, do you? Very well, I've no objection. I'd be quite glad to know where that staircase did run. But you must use reading-glasses. I won't have you strain your eyesight over that crabbed writing, either of you.'

'Very well,' agreed Jesanne. 'It may be easier to tell what the letters are supposed to be, anyhow.'

'I should think that might be quite likely. Have you any more tea there, Jesanne? I'm thirsty this afternoon. The ham is a little on the salty side.'

Jesanne poured out the tea, and the talk passed to other things. But once the meal was ended, and they had washed up and seen that everything was in order, the pair fairly hustled Sir Ambrose off the premises. They raced him across the park through the thick December dusk at a breathless rate, and when they changed, it was only the fear of his looking that made them take time to make themselves even decently tidy. But at last they were ready, and then they raced downstairs, long-legged Lois leading the way, and pranced along to the library, where they found that he had set the great tome on a table under a reading-lamp, and had two reading-glasses waiting for them.

'There you are!' he said. 'Here are two chairs for you. Hello!

What's that for?' as Jesanne produced a pencil and an exercise-book.

'It's only my history-book. I thought we'd write it down as we made it out. It would save a lot of bother later on.'

Sir Ambrose considered. 'Very well. But when you've finished with it, please destroy it. We've never allowed the Journall to be copied. By the way, did you say your history exercise-book? What will Miss Mercier say to that?'

'I can get another, can't I?'

'You can. But I think she would want to know why you had used up the other without permission.'

'Well, you give it to me,' coaxed Jesanne.

'No, I don't think I can do that. But I'll give you another book instead. Wait a moment.' He left them to go into the study, whence he presently returned with a stoutly bound old ledger. 'Here you are. This ledger was bought a good many years ago, and then it was discovered that half the pages were not lined, so it was put aside. You can have it for your work. It's stronger than the flimsy things you have for your lessons, and it's very large, so it ought to be sufficient. Now, is *that* everything?'

'Yes, thank you. And thanks ever so much for the ledger. It's just the very thing.'

'Then I'll leave you to get on while I go and change. Don't overtire yourselves. There are plenty of days coming yet.'

He left the library, and the pair set to work. Jesanne had her plan all ready. They were to read through the early part which described the building of the Dragon House. Then they would go on to the days of the first Sir Ambrose, father of Nicholas and Stephen, and then to those of Caspar Gellibrand, who had built the north wing. If they had gained no hint from those records, Jesanne had decided that they must read on up to the time of the Mr Ambrose Gellibrand who had built the south wing, by which time, as her cousin had told her, all trace of the original staircase had been lost.

'And supposing we *still* find nothing? What then?' demanded Lois when this scheme was outlined for her benefit.

'Then we'll have to think of something else. But it'll take us a good time to get through all that,' replied Jesanne.

Lois looked sceptical. But when she had studied the queer writing, she fully agreed with her friend. It would take them ages to read all that, unless the writing very much improved as they went on.

They set to work with their reading-glasses, taking it turn and turn about, and comparing notes carefully on each doubtful word. They read much that was interesting, though it had no connection whatsoever with the staircase; but they dared miss nothing, in case they should get what Lois called 'the teeniest, weeniest nip of a hint.' Incidentally, they gained a valuable insight into the life of those times, though they were unaware of it at the time.

When Sir Ambrose came downstairs again, he found them flushed and bright-eyed, with ten long sentences written in their ledger, and another almost ready for writing, only neither could make anything of one rather important word.

'It might be *anything*!' said Jesanne despairingly. 'Look at it, Cousin Ambrose. What do *you* think it is?'

He looked at it, but was obliged to confess himself beaten. Then he asserted his authority. 'You've done quite enough for one night. Close that ledger, and take it to the fourth right-hand drawer in my desk, Jesanne. Here are the keys. You can keep it there. I'm going to put the Journall away now. Dinner will be ready in a few minutes, and after dinner you are both going to bed.'

'*Both?*' Jesanne looked up quickly.

'Yes; Mrs Jennings can't get back tonight, and she has rung up to ask me if Lois may spend the night here.'

'Oh, how lovely!' Lois clapped her hands.

'Yes; but remember, when you go to bed, you *go* to bed— and to sleep, I hope. But you will spend tomorrow with us, Lois, and if you and Jesanne can contrive to let the baby-house alone for one day, you can come here in the afternoon and go on with your hunt for clues.'

Lois looked quickly at Jesanne. 'What about it, Jesanne?'

'Oh, yes; of course we will. Anyhow, we could go to the lodge in the morning—'

'Not if it's fine,' said Sir Ambrose firmly. 'If it's fine, you'll both ride with me—at least, can you ride, Lois?'

Lois looked shamefaced. 'Only a very little, I'm afraid. But—'

'Then we'll teach you. Oh, you must learn, of course. But how is it you can't ride—a girl who has wandered all over the world as you have?'

'When I was little, my pony threw me, and I—I got afraid to mount. Daddy used to take me before him, so I never really learned.'

'Still afraid?'

Lois looked irresolute. 'I—I don't know.'

'Well, will you trust yourself to me? I will guarantee that the horse I give you wouldn't throw anyone. And I will be beside you all the time until you feel really sure of sticking on. So will you try?'

She flushed. 'I—I'll try. Truly I will. But I don't think I'll ever be able to ride really well.'

'Nonsense!' said Sir Ambrose. 'You'll be riding as well as Jesanne does in six months' time if you will really trust me.'

Jesanne, who had gone to the office to put away the ledger, returned in time to hear this. 'Doesn't Lois ride?' she asked dismayedly. 'Oh! And I'd been planning some gorgeous rides!'

'She's going to learn,' said Sir Ambrose. 'If it's fine tomorrow, she'll begin. Now, there goes the gong. Come along in to dinner.'

Dinner was a jolly meal, for Sir Ambrose had no notion of allowing Lois to brood over the future. He began to tell the girls stories of the family, and after dinner kept them with him for another hour instead of sending them off as he had said. By the time half-past nine came, both were sleepy, and when they finally got to bed, Lois was so drowsy that she could scarcely answer the cheerful 'Good night, Lois!' which came from Jesanne's bed to the pretty one set up for her in a corner of the great room. She snuggled down under the bedclothes, slipped her hand under her cheek, and fell asleep at once, to dream that she was riding a camel in a point-to-point, which seemed to lead up the lost stairs, straight to Jesanne's lodge, that had, rather surprisingly, moved to the tops of Three Oaks. She was racing against various members of the Gellibrand family and Miss Mercier, who was attired only in long grey hair—how shocked Miss Mercier would have been could she have known it!—and she knew that she simply must beat them all, as only in that way could they ever know why Nicholas Gellibrand had decided for Parliament. They tore on and on, the stairs seeming to extend the whole way, while Jesanne, in the lodge, shrieked 'Scotland for ever!' at the top of her voice. Miss Mercier was just overtaking her, when the camel slipped a foot, and away they all went rolling down the stairs, which folded up after them, leaving Jesanne on the tree-tops, laughing madly. Down and down they rolled, and suddenly wound up at the foot of the stairs—which promptly vanished—with a bump. Lois awoke to find that the faint light of a late December morning was filtering in through the window, and she herself, in a wild tangle of sheets, blankets, counterpane and eiderdown, had tumbled out of bed with a bump that had wakened Jesanne, who was sitting up, giggling wildly at her startled face.

Chapter XV

THE FIRST HINT

THE day had broken grey and still, with a heavy sky and no hint of the sun. A dreary wind moaned through the leafless branches of the trees, and altogether the outlook was dismal. The two girls dressed before the bright wood fire Agnes had lit some time before, with many a look at the dull prospect, and voiced wonder as to what the weather was going to do. It was certainly not going to be fine.

'Look at those queer clouds,' said Lois from the window where she was standing, brushing her curls. She pointed to some yellowish clouds which were slowly creeping up across the sky.

Jesanne finished knotting her tie and came to look. 'Snow! Clouds like that always meant snow at home. I expect it's the same here. Oh, good! If only it's heavy enough we can have some fun! But I don't think you'll get much of a riding lesson at that rate, Lois. What a shame! And I do so want you to learn, because then we can see so much of the country. There are some glorious rides round here.'

Lois flushed. 'You'll think me an awful coward, but I really am afraid of it, Jesanne. I can never forget falling off Pip when I was tiny. It was a horrid feeling, rolling off like that, and not able to save myself at all.'

'Were you hurt?' asked Jesanne, who had made an end of her dressing and was just kneeling down to say her prayers.

'I was rather badly bruised, and I strained a wrist. And then

THE FIRST HINT

I screamed so when Daddy put me up again that Mummy lifted me down at once, and said I wasn't to be teased. I remember it quite well.'

Jesanne dropped to her knees. 'It was a pity in one way. Now I'm going to say my prayers, so don't talk for a minute or two, please.'

Lois followed her example, and then they tossed back their bedclothes, opened the windows, and left the room. As they reached the Angel Gallery, Lois looked up at the carving with interested eyes.

'How wonderful it is! Yes; I don't think anyone *would* cover it up! What did you mean by saying it's a pity they didn't make me ride again?'

'Auntie Anne told me,' began Jesanne, 'if a thing like that happens to you, it's best to try again at once, or you might lose your nerve. You did, you see. Now it's ten times harder to start again. She made me try again with my bicycle when I fell off. She said if I gave up, I'd only find it worse the next day. So I tried, and she kept beside me to see I didn't have too bad a tumble, and I learned to keep up in three days. Oh, I've had falls since, but I've never been afraid of them, though some have been quite nasty. Now if your people had insisted, you'd have stuck on next time—you can always hug your horse's neck, you know, if the worst comes to the worst—and you'd be able to ride by this time. But don't be scared. Cousin Ambrose will look after you. And if it's Red Robin he's giving you, riding him is like riding a chair. He's a dear!'

Lois laughed. 'If it's like that, I'll try to be plucky. Anyhow,' she added more cheerfully, 'I was riding a camel all night, and up the lost staircase too. It can't be worse than that.'

Jesanne stared at her. 'What are you talking about?'

'My dream. Oh, Jesanne, it was the silliest thing!' And then she told it to Jesanne, who dropped down on the stairs to rock with mirth over the vision of Miss Mercier as told by Lois.

'But you'd better not tell *her* anything about it,' she warned her chum when at length she could speak. 'She'd be dreadfully shocked.'

'Are you two coming to breakfast today or tomorrow?' asked Sir Ambrose from the foot of the stairs. 'We must get off as soon after as possible. We're going to have a snowstorm, I'm afraid.'

The pair ran down the remaining stairs to the morning-room where breakfast was always served, and Sir Ambrose hurried them through it. Like Jesanne, he thought it a pity that Lois's parents had not made her persevere with her riding, and he was determined to see that she rode well and fearlessly before long. Prayers followed breakfast, and then the girls were sent upstairs to change into jodhpurs—a pair that had belonged to Gwen Gellibrand had been unearthed for long-legged Lois—and presently they were down in the stable-yard, watching as Rufa, Tomtit, and Red Robin were led out. Sir Ambrose put Jesanne up, and then turned to Lois.

'Now, Lois, I'm going to lift you on to Robin. Don't be afraid. He's very gentle, and you'll be perfectly safe. I'll walk beside you at present.' He slipped Tomtit's reins over his arm after he had lifted Lois to Robin's back, and began leading the gentle beasts out of the yard, Jesanne following on Rufa, who felt skittish and proceeded by a series of dancing steps that made Lois exclaim in alarm.

'Take Rufa on, and give her a canter, Jesanne,' said her cousin. 'She's full of corn. Now, Lois, take up the reins properly—like this, do you see?' He put the reins in her fingers, and, resisting a desire to fling her arms round Robin's neck, Lois took them, and even managed to sit up erect.

'Good girl!' said Sir Ambrose approvingly. 'Now don't be afraid; you're perfectly safe. Grip the saddle with your knees. That's right. We'll just walk at present.'

Clinging with her knees like grim death, Lois felt the great muscles ripple along Robin's back and loins as he walked down the path. Jesanne was out of sight, having given Rufa her head, and was enjoying a tearing gallop over the withered-looking grass. Sir Ambrose led the horses on to the grass, and for some time walked up and down, leading Robin and Tomtit, and encouraging Lois with praise as she tried to keep a straight back, hold her hands down, and let Robin feel his head.

Presently Jesanne came cantering back, Rufa slightly blown after that mad gallop. 'Well done, Lois!' she cried. 'You do look nice! You'll soon be able to ride—won't she, Cousin Ambrose?'

'Yes, she will,' said Sir Ambrose decidedly. 'Now, Lois, do you think you can bear it if I mount and lead you? Tomtit is very quiet, as you must have seen, and won't excite Robin.'

Lois gave a little gasp. Then she set her jaw. '*Yes!*' she said tersely.

He nodded. 'Brave girl! Here, Jesanne; take the reins a moment.'

Jesanne took the reins while he mounted, and then, with one on each side of her, Lois made her first attempt at riding alone. It was not so bad, after all. Sir Ambrose was careful to go at a walk, and presently Lois found that she was forgetting to feel afraid and beginning to enjoy the movement. But her host took care that she should not be over-tested. After twenty minutes of it, he turned the horses and made for the Dragon House.

'That's enough for one day,' he said. 'I don't want you to be too stiff, Lois. If it's fine tomorrow, you shall try again. You've done very well for a first time.'

'I—I like it,' said Lois shyly. 'I'm sorry, now, I didn't try at once after my fall. Then I might have been riding properly by this time.'

'Never mind,' he said cheerily. 'Better late than never! Ah! Here comes the snow! It'll be whirling down presently.' For a flake or two had fallen as he spoke, and the sky was heavily overcast.

They reached the stable-yard without mishap, and Sir Ambrose sent the two girls in at once, promising to see to the comfort of the horses himself for once. They ran in, and hurried upstairs to change back into skirts and make themselves tidy. Then they went down to the library, where they found him sitting by the fire, looking over the Christmas Eve morning papers. Their table had been set out, ready for them, and a tray with hot chocolate and buns was also waiting.

'Good!' cried Jesanne. 'I'm ravenous! Oo-ooh! Look at the snow! How it's coming down!'

It was, as Cousin Ambrose had foretold, whirling madly earthwards, and the girls, after they had drunk their chocolate and munched their buns, turned back thankfully to the cosy library, and settled down at the table.

Work went better today. Perhaps the exercise in the open air had sharpened their brains. Perhaps the writing was just a little improved. At any rate, when the gong sounded for lunch they had quite a good deal of writing to their credit, though they had come on no hint as to how the staircase had vanished.

'Still,' said Jesanne, as they went into the dining-room, 'we do know that there was one, though it doesn't say very clearly where it was.'

After lunch they settled down to work again, and this time Lois was inspired to suggest that they should skip a little and go to the later days. Jesanne was quite agreeable; so they passed over a good deal, and finally came to the pages which told of the

THE FIRST HINT

death of old Sir Ambrose of Civil War times, and the accession of his son Stephen to the property.

Sir Stephen Gellibrand seemed to have been no hand at writing. His statements were curt, not to say bald, and Jesanne sighed impatiently for what he *might* have written about that stirring epoch if only he had had the pen of a ready writer.

'Oh, bother all that!' retorted Lois in answer to her lamentations. 'We want to find out about the staircase—oh, look here, Jesanne! Here's something!'

'Where?' Jesanne crowded her smooth black head below Lois's curls, and read—slowly, perforce—the following thrilling extract: 'Jany. 14th 1652. This day came home my brother Nicholas that my father did cast forth when he met him on the staircase having papers in his hands, and saying that he could not fight for any king that so misused his subjects as did his late lamented Majesty, whereat my sire flew into a right royal rage, and did bid Nick betake himself hence, for no Gellibrand that should be so disloyal should remain in the Dragon House.'

(Needless to state, this was not spelt as I have written it down, but spelling of those times is not always easy to follow.)

'So it was on the staircase that it happened,' said Jesanne.

'Oh, yes,' said Sir Ambrose, looking up from his leading article. 'We have always known that. That, Jesanne, is one of the last references to the staircase.'

'I believe we're on the track!' Jesanne's eyes were bright with excitement. 'Come on, Lois! Let's read on a bit.'

They read on, and were interested in Stephen's account of the scene between Nicholas and Cromwell. But they found no more about the staircase there. They went on to read about the letter coming from Jesanne's ancestress, and how Nicholas had been sent off to bring her to the Dragon House. Sir Ambrose tossed aside his paper and came to join them, now as interested as they.

'Skip all that,' ordered Jesanne when they left Nicholas and his errand, and came on Stephen's account of how the salted meat was likely to serve for the winter. 'We can come back to it.'

'But isn't it interesting!' cried Lois.

Sir Ambrose glanced at her. 'Keen on history, eh?' he asked.

'I wasn't,' confessed Lois. 'But this makes it all so *alive* somehow. Fancy having nothing but salted meat all the winter!'

'Still, that isn't what we're looking for now,' pointed out Jesanne reasonably. 'We'll come back to it later, Lois.'

Sir Ambrose turned the pages slowly, giving them time to look at each one in case any mention of the staircase should have been made. For eight pages it was never named. Then, just as he was about to turn to the ninth, Jesanne gave a cry, and pushed his hand away.

'Wait a minute! There's something here!'

He let the page fall, as excited as they, and the three heads bent over the quaintly archaic writing while Jesanne read aloud: '"Last night a branch from the—" What's that? I can't make it out.'

They puzzled over a word that looked like nothing any of them had ever seen before.

'That's an "E,"' said Lois positively. 'Look; there's the two outside strokes, and that squiggle in the middle must be the middle. It's like a capital E written wrong—or scrawly, anyhow.'

'Then that's an "L,"' declared Sir Ambrose. 'And this must be another.'

'And here's another "E"! But what *is* the weird scrawl after it?' Jesanne looked anxiously at them.

'It looks—like—a "Z,"' said Lois, knitting her brows.

'It *couldn't* be! Whatever tree is spelt "E, L, L, E, Z"?' asked Jesanne.

They studied the queer word. Then Sir Ambrose solved the mystery.

'That's not a "Z." It's intended for an "M." There you are—Stephen's spelling of the word "Elm"!'

'Of course! How stupid not to think of it at once! I'll go on, shall I?' Jesanne read the word, and then went on, '"that grows beside the great window broke and fell, one end breaking the glass, and scattering it on the broad staircase where Dame Alice found it in the—the morning"—Is that it? It looks more like that than anything else.' She appealed to her cousin.

'That's most probably right. Go on, Jesanne.'

'"I have ordered that it be swept ere the bairns cut their fingers playing with it. But this decides me that the broad staircase hath served its day, and needs must I build that which my good sire planned ere all the troubles came."'

'There you are!' cried Lois. 'We know that the staircase was there then, and Stephen meant to build another—I suppose the one that's there now.'

'He certainly didn't build *that*,' said Sir Ambrose. 'It is of at least twenty years' later date than 1652. I've always been under the impression that his son, Caspar, was responsible for it. That's the family tradition, anyhow.'

Jesanne was turning the page. Suddenly, she gave a cry. 'Cousin Ambrose! This page is thicker than the others! Why?'

He bent forward quickly to examine; but by this time it was dark. He hurried to the bell, and rang a peal that brought Totton in double-quick time to the library, to be sent hurriedly for the lamps. When they were brought, they were set round, and then Sir Ambrose carefully examined the extra-thick page.

'I know!' he said at length. 'I'm sorry to disappoint you people, but this is only a flaw in the paper. Paper was made of rags in those days, as you know. Something must have gone wrong with this sheet.—Why, Jesanne!' For that young lady had leapt from her chair and torn from the room without a word of explanation.

She was back almost as soon as she was gone, bringing with her a tiny electric torch. 'Hold the page up, Cousin Ambrose!' she said breathlessly. 'Move that lamp, Lois.'

Wonderingly, they obeyed her. She set the torch against the leaf so that the light shone through. Sir Ambrose saw what she would be at, and bent his head beside hers. For a moment there was silence. Then he spoke again.

'Take the torch, Lois! Now, Jesanne; look carefully.'

Jesanne looked.

'Oh, what *is* it?' wailed Lois, nearly wild with curiosity.

'Give me the torch, and come and see,' he said.

Lois handed him the torch, and then pressed her curly head against Jesanne's. For a moment there was silence. Then a gasp sounded through the room.

'It *is*—oh, it *is*!' cried Jesanne. 'Someone has pasted or glued two pages together. Oh, how can we get them unstuck?'

Chapter XVI

'Patience is a Virtue'

It was a difficult question. Once Sir Ambrose was certain that Jesanne's sense of touch had not deceived her, he was as anxious as any of them to find out what lay between those two sealed pages. It was quite certain that there was writing. Their experiments with the torch had settled that. But the problem was how to part the pages without harm to either paper or ink.

'Sponge them with warm water,' suggested Lois.

'Then the ink would run,' said Jesanne.

'I'm afraid it wouldn't do,' agreed her cousin. 'For one thing, the paper is very old. For another, whatever was used to stick them together like this is of long standing, and I doubt if sponging will dissolve it. Besides, we want the surfaces left intact.'

'Then what are we to do?' asked Jesanne impatiently.

'Nothing—I mean for the present,' he added soothingly as he saw the horrified expressions on the two small faces before him. 'I must have an expert down—'

'Oh, *no!*' wailed Jesanne. 'If you do, then *he'll* be the first to know what happened, and I'm sure it ought to be one of the family.'

'There's something in that,' he said thoughtfully. 'At the same time, Jesanne, I don't see what else we are to do.'

Lois had been looking puzzled. 'Isn't there some kind of photography they do nowadays, so that they can read writing *under* writing?' she asked suddenly. 'I've heard Daddy talk about it. It's got a special name—*you* know, Sir Ambrose.'

But Sir Ambrose did *not* know. Photography was no hobby of his, and he had no idea what she was talking about. Still, it was an idea, and he promised the excited girls that he would write to some big photographers' firm in London, and see if he could find out anything about Lois's idea.

'When will you do it?' demanded Jesanne.

'This evening, before the post-bag goes—ah! This is Boxing Day. It won't go off till tomorrow, then. But I will have it ready, and Rees can take it with him when he goes for the bag,' said Sir Ambrose.

'All that time to wait! You can't possibly get an answer for three days at soonest. Oh *dear*!'

Jesanne's face was very long as she gazed at him and Lois, and Lois was not far behind. Sir Ambrose laughed at them.

'The secret has been kept for more than two hundred years. A few days more or less won't make so much difference. In the meantime, we might see if we can learn anything more from the Journall. Hand me that bookmark, Jesanne, and we'll mark the place. Now we'll go on, Lois; it's your turn to make a discovery, I think.'

But though they looked carefully at half a dozen more pages, they found nothing that had any bearing on the family mystery, and when Totton and his coadjutor came in with tea, they were glad to lay the great tome aside for the present.

After tea, Sir Ambrose sent them to play in the big billiard-room with the dogs, saying that they had pored over the Journall quite long enough for one day, and Mr Jennings arrived at half-past six to retrieve his visitor.

'It's Lois's turn to entertain Jesanne,' he said, as he slipped an arm round his niece's shoulders. 'May she come down to us for the day tomorrow, Sir Ambrose?'

'A very good thing,' said Sir Ambrose cordially. 'But I hope you will bring Lois over first at about ten. I've begun to teach her to ride, as Jesanne wants a young companion for her rides. She had her first lesson today, and ought to have another tomorrow—weather permitting.'

'If it's decent weather, I'll bring her with pleasure,' returned Mr Jennings. 'But, unless I'm much mistaken, this storm will last a while yet. So in that case, may Jesanne come to us about eleven? We will send her back safely at about seven in the evening if that will do?'

'Splendidly,' said Sir Ambrose, paying no heed to the downfallen looks of the two girls. 'Jesanne, you will enjoy that, won't you?'

Thus reminded of her manners, Jesanne had to come forward and thank Mr Jennings as prettily as she could for his invitation, and say that she would love to spend the day with Lois. But neither of them was too keen on it. They wanted to be together: but they wanted to go on with the Journall. This was just what Sir Ambrose was anxious to avoid. He didn't want them to strain their eyesight or tire themselves with excitement over it. A day's rest would be all to the good.

So they had to put up with it. And once they had got over their disappointment, they managed to enjoy themselves very well. In the afternoon Mrs Jennings, who was a slender, pretty woman, full of fun, and not so very old—she was only thirty-three as a matter of fact—took them into the kitchen, and showed them how to make fudge, peppermint creams, and sundry other sweets. They were so thrilled with their own concoctions that they contrived to forget their search for the lost staircase for the time being; and when Jesanne said goodbye to her kind hostess, she was able truthfully to assure her that she had had a very jolly time.

'You must come again in a few days' time,' said Mrs Jennings. She bent and kissed the child with that look in her eyes which told those who knew that her little lost daughter was never far from her thoughts. Then she closed the car-door, and Jesanne was whirled off to the Dragon House through a world of white that looked silver under the cold light of the winter stars.

The next morning Sir Ambrose told Jesanne at breakfast that he was going up to London for the day. 'I've rung up the Jennings,' he said, 'and Lois will come up about ten. Why not spend the day at your cottage? Agnes can go down with you, and you can take the dogs. I shan't be home again till late, so you will have to go to bed at your usual time, and look forward to hearing all my news tomorrow.'

Jesanne looked at him quickly. 'News? Oh, will it be about the Journall?' she pleaded.

He laughed. 'You must wait till tomorrow, little maid.'

'If you say so, I suppose I must,' sighed Jesanne. Then she brightened. 'Come up and see if I'm asleep, Cousin Ambrose. I mightn't be. Oh, *do*!'

'If you will promise me not to try to keep awake, I might do that.'

'I'll promise. I'm sure I shan't be asleep, though.'

'Well, we'll see.'

He left her presently, to get ready for his trip to Town, and she waved goodbye to him from the doorstep.

'Goodbye, Cousin Ambrose. Take care of yourself, and be back as soon as you can!' she called, as the car began to move.

He waved to her with a smile, thinking that life, even when his best treasures were gone, still held some compensations. He had grown very fond of his little cousin, and it was pleasant to have someone to see him off once more. It recalled the old days. Some day, and he smiled again as he thought of it, she should have the last wish of her heart, and Miss Mortimer should come to stay with them. But not yet. The Gellibrands, as he had truly told her, did not like eating humble pie, and he knew that he must apologise for his treatment of an unknown lady before she would consent to accept his hospitality.

Left to herself, Jesanne turned to seek Spike and ask her for provisions for the day. She was a great favourite with the household by this time, and the housekeeper, with a beaming smile, promised to fill a basket for her.

'I'm taking the dogs,' said Jesanne. 'Cousin Ambrose said so. Will you see to Little Tommy for me, please? He isn't very friendly with them yet, so I can't take him with me, though I'd like to.'

'Never you fear, Miss Jesanne,' said Mrs Spike. 'I'll look after your cat. Now run along, and mind you wrap up warm. 'Tis bitter cold today.'

Jesanne skipped off, and presently she and Agnes, accompanied by the four house-dogs, were making their way over the slippery snow to the south lodge, each carrying a basket. Jesanne had rung up the Jennings, and Mr Jennings had promised to bring Lois straight to the cottage.

Someone had gone down early by order of Sir Ambrose, and the fires were glowing in the kitchen and the parlour. Jesanne discarded her wraps in the little briar-rose bedroom, and donned a pinafore, and then ran downstairs to seek dusters and brooms and set to work to reduce her little domain to a state of perfect neatness. Lois arrived while she was still busy, and after a rapturous greeting the pair finished the work, peeled the potatoes and prepared the sprouts for lunch, and then wrapped themselves up again to take the dogs for a romp outside, Agnes undertaking to see to the cooking of the vegetables. Mrs Spike had sent some slices of cold lamb, and there were mince-pies for a second course, so no other cooking was necessary.

After a wild frolic, in which the two girls got thoroughly untidy, and even old Beowulf forgot his years and his dignity and played like a young dog, they all came in, glowing and hungry with exercise. Agnes had laid lunch in the little parlour, and Carver had walked down with the dogs' dinner, and they all fell to with gargantuan appetites. When it was over, and everything was washed up and put tidily away, Agnes settled down to her knitting in the kitchen, and the two girls, with the tired dogs, cuddled down on the couch in the parlour, and indulged in much wondering as to what could be hidden between those sealed pages.

'Perhaps it's an account of where the family plate was hidden during the Civil War,' suggested Lois the romantic.

'It couldn't be. We've *got* all the family plate—at least, I think so,' returned Jesanne the matter-of-fact.

'Well, perhaps they had to hide Lady Gellibrand's jewels and things to save them from the Roundheads.' Lois was loath to give up her idea.

'I should think it's much more likely it's something about the lost staircase,' said Jesanne.

'But *why* should anyone want to stick that up?'

'I don't know. There may have been a good reason. Oh, I do wish we hadn't to wait so long. But I'm nearly sure that's why Cousin Ambrose has gone up to London, so we should know fairly soon now.'

'Well, mind you're awake when he comes home. And if it's anything about that, get him to let you ring me up,' said Lois. 'I know I shall be awake, because I'll be longing—'

Her speech was interrupted by a heavy knock at the door. The two started to their feet.

'Who on earth can that be?' exclaimed Jesanne.

'A tramp, perhaps,' suggested Lois.

They were answered by the appearance of Agnes, followed by Mr Jennings. Lois exclaimed at sight of him.

'Why, Uncle Reggie! Have you come to tea?'

'PATIENCE IS A VIRTUE'

He sat down. 'No, dear. I have a message for Jesanne.'

'For me?' Jesanne turned wondering eyes on him.

'Yes, dear. Jesanne, can you be very plucky?'

'Oh, what has happened?' Jesanne's cry rang sharply through the twilit room.

He set his hands on her shoulders, and held her before him. 'Steady, Jesanne! It's that Sir Ambrose has met with an accident and broken his leg.'

'Oh, poor Cousin Ambrose! How awful!' Jesanne, luckily, did not understand how dangerous a broken leg might be to a man of Sir Ambrose's age, and Mr Jennings did not enlighten her.

'Yes; it's pretty bad. Mercifully, it was a clean break. He was taken to a near-by nursing home, where they've set it, and he hopes to get home in a week or two. In the meantime, he has asked us—Mrs Jennings and me—to come to the Dragon House to take charge while he is absent. We can't manage it for a couple of days; but we'll come on New Year's Eve, and for the time being Lois shall stay with you.'

'But—Cousin Ambrose? Is he in London? Can't I go to him?'

'Not yet, dear. He has to be kept very quiet for a day or two. Such an accident is a shock for a man of his age, you know. But next week, if all is well, I'll take you up to Town and you shall spend an hour with him.'

'Is he badly ill?' asked Jesanne, looking scared.

'Well, he's not feeling very fit, naturally. But the doctors are satisfied with him in the circumstances, and that's all anyone can say at this stage.'

Jesanne nodded. 'Poor Cousin Ambrose! Oh, it is hard lines! And just when we'd made such jolly plans for the holidays!'

'How did it happen, Uncle Reggie?' asked Lois, who had kept silence up to this moment.

He looked stern. 'Through someone's wicked carelessness. He

had just stepped out of the car, and he slipped on a banana-skin, and fell, doubling his leg under him. If only people would realise how much harm they do by throwing banana-skins and orange-peel about the streets, they would stop it, and there wouldn't be half the bad street accidents one hears about. Never let me catch *you* doing such a thing, Lois.'

'I never would! Why, Mummy and Daddy would have a fit if they thought I did!' cried Lois indignantly.

He smiled slightly. 'I suppose so. Well, Auntie Meg has sent up a case with your things, and we'll bring the rest when we come. Now, Jesanne, I must be getting home again. I'm going on to the Dragon House to tell the household what has happened. You and Lois are to spend the night here, so Agnes will come with me, and bring what you need. You'll be far better in this cosy little crib than up at the big house, won't you? Your cousin suggested it himself.'

'He said that we might sleep here if we had the dogs and Agnes to keep us company,' said Jesanne soberly.

'I know. So that will be all right.' He rose to go, but Jesanne detained him.

'Please, Mr Jennings, have you *seen* Cousin Ambrose?'

'Yes; they rang me up by his orders, once he had come out of the anaesthetic—'

'Anaesthetic!' Jesanne's voice was full of horror.

'Of course, he had to have something to deaden the pain of having his leg set. Why, you silly child, you look ready to cry. *I* had an anaesthetic when they set my collar-bone last year. It's always done.'

Jesanne drew a long breath. 'I didn't mean to be silly, but it sounded so frightening. How does he look?' Then she added rather piteously, 'He's all I've got in England, you know.'

Mr Jennings considered his answer carefully. 'He didn't look his fittest. You wouldn't expect that with a broken leg, would you? But he was as comfortable as they could make him, and he sent his love to you, and told me to tell you to remember that patience is a virtue, and you must just practise it for a little.'

They let him go after that, and he departed to tell the Dragon House household what had befallen their master, and warn them to say nothing to frighten Jesanne. He himself knew that there is always a risk of pneumonia after such an accident to a man of Sir Ambrose's age. He had not dared to speak too cheerfully about it to the child; but he was determined that she should not be worried by the fear if he could help it.

'I hope it will all go well with him, Meg,' he said to his wife late that evening when they were sitting in their pretty drawing-room together. He had just come back from the south lodge, where, in an interview with the faithful Agnes, he had learnt that the two girls had gone to bed at nine o'clock, and were now fast asleep.

Mrs Jennings looked anxious. 'I thought you said it was a clean break?'

'So it is. But with a man of his age—and after all he has undergone this past few years—'

'But he has looked very much better lately, Reggie.'

'Oh, yes. There's no doubt about it. The coming of that child has given him a fresh interest. But none of us can hope to defeat anno domini. Still, he has a magnificent constitution, and has led a quiet, regular life, and that's all in his favour. The doctor told me that if he got through the next two or three days safely, humanly speaking he would be safe. They're afraid he'll always limp slightly, though. Old bones don't knit like young ones.'

'Oh, I hope he comes through!' breathed Mrs Jennings, clasping her hands. 'It would be so terrible for that poor child if he went.'

'Don't you be afraid, Meg. He told me that he meant to get well as fast as possible. I believe it will be all right. He has the will to live, and that's half the battle, as any doctor will tell you. If this had happened even six months ago, I shouldn't have had much hope. As it is, what with the child, and this new excitement about finding some clue to that lost staircase of theirs, I expect we shall have him among us in a few weeks' time, no worse for all this.'

'Except the limp,' said Mrs Jennings softly.

'He'll put up with that.'

'Yes; he has known worse troubles. Oh, how thankful I am that little Jesanne is here. She will be the magnet to draw him back to life again!'

Chapter XVII

The Search Continues

Happily for everyone, Sir Ambrose did not develop pneumonia, and he was soon going on as satisfactorily as possible, though the knitting of the broken bone seemed likely to be a long process. As soon as he was able to bear it, Mr Jennings took Jesanne up to the nursing home to visit him, and thereafter she went once a week, greatly to the satisfaction of both. The doctors refused to let the patient return home until six weeks were up, so by the time he was brought back to the Dragon House in triumph, Miss Mercier had returned, and lessons were in full swing.

The addition of Lois to the schoolroom was a source of much satisfaction to Jesanne, whatever the governess might think about it. To have a fellow-sufferer made Miss Mercier's somewhat overbearing treatment easier to endure: but, as a matter of fact, she had changed during the holidays in a rather amazing manner. She seemed absent and distracted at times, and she certainly overlooked much that before Christmas would have brought trouble on the heads of the schoolroom pair. Jesanne set it down to being away from the dogs, and thought no more about it.

Sir Ambrose had issued strict orders that lessons were to occupy only the mornings. The rest of the day the girls were to spend in walking and, as soon as Lois could manage it, riding. Hiles, who was both head-groom and chauffeur, undertook Lois's tuition. He was as careful as Sir Ambrose himself, and once she had got control of her nerves, the girl made rapid progress. When it was too wet to go out, the two amused themselves at the south lodge, accompanied by Agnes, the dogs, and Little Tommy, who was growing fast, and, as Jesanne declared, would be a credit to his mother. He kept the dogs in order, permitting no liberties, and it was funny to see how the black scrap of long wool soon 'bossed' his own particular pup, Sanchia. They ate from the same dish, played together with the same ball, and the cold nights found Little Tommy sharing Sanchia's basket, curled up against her. When she became too boisterous, he boxed her ears with paddy paws that could slap hard, and generally kept her in order.

Miss Mercier had looked a trifle sour at the new addition to the party, but, warned by Sir Ambrose's attitude towards the dogs, she said nothing. Besides, the Jennings were in full control until the master of the house came back, and they were as determined as he that the girls should grow up with animals.

It meant, of course, that there was little time for work at the Journall. In addition to her other lessons, Jesanne had resumed her 'cello, and she had to put in a couple of hours' practice every day, for her master was strict. Lois, too, had a violin, so after tea she adjourned to the schoolroom, while Jesanne went to the drawing-room, and both practised hard.

But at length the joyous day came when Sir Ambrose, complete with the crutches he hoped soon to cast aside, was brought back to the Dragon House, and the next day the Jennings returned to the Manor House, and Lois, of course, went with them.

'It's so nice to have you back, Cousin Ambrose,' said Jesanne that evening after dinner, when they were sitting in the library. 'I've missed you horribly.'

He glanced across at her with a smile. 'That's pleasant hearing, little maid. But I'm sure Mr and Mrs Jennings were very good to you. And you've had Lois as well.'

'Oh, yes. But one wants one's own people,' said Jesanne thoughtfully.

'Yes; I suppose so. Well, how has the search gone on all this time? Got any further?'

She shook her head. 'Not much. We've read where Mr Ambrose says that he can't find any trace of the old staircase, nor where it used to run. But there really isn't much about it. And we've not had so much time, either.'

'Not had too much preparation, have you?' he asked quickly.

'Oh, no. Miss Mercier has set very little. But there's our music, of course. And then we have our Latin twice a week— Oh, Cousin Ambrose, it's so nice that Lois is up to me in Latin! We can work together beautifully.'

'I'm glad to hear that.'

Jesanne left her chair, pulled up a stool, and sat close beside him. 'Cousin Ambrose, it really was a good thing you gave Miss Mercier the west lodge to live in. It seems to have made a big difference to her. She's not nearly so—so *difficult* as she was last term.'

He gave a chuckle. 'I don't think *that* has had much to do with it. Don't you know what's happened?'

'Happened? Why, what could happen? Cousin Ambrose, what *do* you mean?'

'Hasn't Miss Mercier told you, then, that she is to be married in July?'

'Married—Miss Mercier?' Jesanne's astonishment was by no means complimentary to her governess. 'Who ever would want to *marry* her?'

'Oh, come, Jesanne! Miss Mercier is a handsome woman. She is dignified, and will make an excellent wife in many ways. She is marrying an old friend whom she met again during the holidays. He is a doctor—a specialist in London—and I should say she was just the wife for him.'

Jesanne ruminated on the surprising statement for a moment

or two in silence. 'When in July will she be married?' she asked.

'I believe during the first week. I don't know that the date is definitely fixed. By the way, she asked me if you might be her bridesmaid.'

'Oh—*need* I?' Jesanne's tones were full of pleading.

'It means a new kit. Also, a nice present from the bridegroom, though I don't suppose you care for that much.'

'I *don't*! What ever made her pitch on me? I'd heaps rather not.'

'Well, we needn't arrange anything till nearer the time,' said Sir Ambrose soothingly. 'I've already told her that I can say nothing about it for the present. We may be away for the summer—I don't know. In the meantime, suppose you and Lois do your best to give the lady as little trouble as possible. She's leaving us at the end of May, as she wants a few weeks to get ready. That's not quite five months' time. Do give her a good impression, Jesanne.'

'It's only *four* months,' Jesanne reminded him. 'This is February.'

'So it is.'

'And there's the Easter holidays out of that. If she goes on as she has been doing we can put up with her. But are we to have holidays from May onwards, then?'

'I expect so. You can start fair again in September. Besides, you won't be left to run wild, either of you. Lois is coming here for the whole of June, and I shall have—a lady to take care of you two.'

Sir Ambrose spoke in a peculiar tone, but Jesanne was too absorbed in the news about Lois to notice it.

'The whole of June? Oh, Cousin Ambrose, how lovely! Of course, I see her every day; but it'll be heaps better having her all the time. Are the Jennings going away, then?'

'No; but they will be very much occupied. Lois will be better here. And now, Jesanne, don't you want to hear what I've done about Lois's suggestion of photographing the pages?'

'I thought you'd forgotten,' said Jesanne. 'Your accident—and all the horrid pain—I didn't expect you'd have time to think of it.'

'Well, I hadn't at first. And then I put off for a little till I could attend to it personally. However, I saw an old friend, Professor Gresley, two days ago. He is interested in all sorts of science, but his pet subject is electricity. He knew at once what she had meant when I mentioned it to him.'

'What luck! And what is it? Can it be done?'

'It's done by what are called the infra-red rays—now don't ask me to explain *that* to you, for I can't. I'm no scientist. But it seems they use a special kind of camera, and, very especially, a particular kind of photographic plate which is peculiarly sensitised. Gresley was very much interested in what I told him. He has made rather a hobby of this kind of work, and he is coming down in three weeks' time to photograph the page, and any others that seem to be thicker than the rest, just in case they have been treated the same way.'

'How frightfully thrilling! Why, we may get all sorts of information from it. Oh, Cousin Ambrose, it's too exciting for words! But—*three weeks*! Can't it be sooner? It's such a long time to wait.'

'Gresley can't get away sooner. And, as I told you before, it's already waited so long, a little longer won't hurt. In any case,' he added warningly, 'there may be nothing about the staircase, you know. Don't build too much on it, Jesanne.'

'Oh, I won't. But somehow I feel there'll be *some*thing—even if it's only a hint.'

'Well, there may be. In the meantime, we'll go on looking through the Journall. Lois may stay to tea tomorrow, and after tea we'll have another go at it. I suppose you haven't been doing it while I was away?'

'Mrs Jennings didn't give us much chance. She said she'd rather we left the Journall alone until you came. Besides, she's been teaching us to knit jumpers for ourselves. Want to see mine? It's nearly finished.'

'Yes; bring it along. But don't knit in here in the evenings,' he added hastily. 'I can't bear the click-click of knitting-needles. Besides, I want you to become a good chess-player. We must have some games, now I'm back.'

Jesanne laughed. 'I'm not so fond of knitting as all that. But Mrs Jennings said we ought to know how. I'll be back in a minute— No, Sanchia! You can't go! Stay here!' For the long-legged pup had bounded to her feet on seeing her little mistress go to the door.

Sanchia turned and went back, tail between her legs, and Jesanne raced off, to return with a woolly, shapeless mass in blue, which she exhibited with much pride. He looked at it, remarked on the pretty colour, and then pushed it aside.

'Well, you can put it away now. I'll see it when you wear it. In the meanwhile, get the cards, and we'll play cribbage till dinner-time.'

Jesanne folded up her work and got the cards, and they settled down till Totton came to announce dinner. After dinner they went back to the library, and Sir Ambrose asked to hear what they had done of the Journall while he had been away, so she got the ledger, and read out what they had done, after which it was her bedtime, and she had to say good-night, once prayers were over.

The next day, remembering that she had done next to no practice at her 'cello the previous day, and that her lesson was on the Friday, Jesanne spent the first part of the afternoon practising, while Lois gave her violin a little attention. But when four o'clock came, and with it tea-time, they were ready to get to work again on the Journall. Sir Ambrose was quite as ready as they, so once tea was over the party adjourned to the library, and they set to work on the pages they had missed that first day together.

They read a great deal about the Civil War, always told as baldly as possible, for Stephen Gellibrand had hated writing of any kind, and only his sense of duty kept him at it. They were interested to learn how 'my lady hath made a new kirtle for little Nann from her old purple wooll gownd, and hath added thereto a tucker of Flemysh lace.' Also, that 'Littell Nann and Mun and Pegge are taken down with the meesels, and Dr Perssysche recommendeth that they bee keeped in a dark chamber, with red coverlid and hangins at the bed to presearve theyre eyne, for it bee well knowen that meessells'—Stephen Gellibrand was not particular about his spelling, much to the delight of his latest descendant!—'doth much harm the eye if childer bee not wel cared.'

'What a queer idea,' ruminated Lois when they had read this.

'It was an old idea that red—the colour of the rash—was a good preventive of trouble in such diseases,' explained Sir Ambrose. 'People with smallpox, for instance, were always kept in a room with red hangings, and red curtains at the windows. I saw some time ago that doctors are beginning to think that our ancestors, though *they* used the treatment largely as a result of the study of astrology and so on, were not so far out. There is no doubt that the reddish light helps to preserve the skin from thickening, which is so often caused by that most horrible of sicknesses.'

'How interesting!' said Jesanne. 'Just fancy those old people knowing all about something-red rays—or anyhow working with them, even if they didn't know what they were doing.'

'Oh, our forefathers knew a good deal,' he said drily. 'Well, let us go on.'

They went on, and discovered that Nann and Pegge were soon

up and running about, but that Mun, who seemed to have been weakly, was ill a long time after his sturdy sisters were done with even 'kitchen physic.'

'That would be Edmund Gellibrand,' said Sir Ambrose thoughtfully. 'He was always a frail mortal, and died at the age of twenty-two, shortly before the outbreak of the Great Plague.'

'Did it come here?' demanded Jesanne.

'Of course it did. Haven't I told you about the huge pit full of bones and other relics discovered at Wyesford when they were doing some excavations near the spot where the old gaol stood? It raged in the city, and in the villages near by. The Dragon House estate escaped, however, largely, I imagine, as a result of being so isolated, even in those days. But it was a terrible time for most of the county.'

'Can't we go on and read what it says about it?' pleaded Lois.

He turned the pages carefully, and at length stopped at one. 'Here you are. Hand me that glass, Jesanne, and I'll read it to you. This,' he added, as he took the glass from her, 'is about three years after the death of Sir Stephen, and was written by his eldest son, Caspar.'

'I thought it looked rather better writing,' commented Jesanne.

'Caspar was a much more scholarly man than his father. Now sit quiet while I read to you.'

The two girls settled themselves, and listened eagerly while he read aloud: '"This day came Thomas Rees to tell me that the Plague be broke out in the city, and already many be dead or dying from it. I have sent him to the east lodge, and bidden him not stir from thence till I give him leave, for I am determined that here we will none of it. My lady hath prepared a mighty bowl of sulphur, and molasses, and herbs, and will dose the household therewith night and morning till all danger be past. Also, I have stablished men at the borders to keep ward, and drive any hence that would cross them."— You see,' he went on, pausing in his reading, 'how careful they were.'

'I think "my lady's medicine" sounds simply horrid,' said Jesanne decidedly.

'No doubt. But plague was worse. It was drastic treatment, but it may very well have contributed to the immunity of the household. Now shall I go on?'

'Oh, yes; please do!' The girls were united in their desire to hear more.

He smiled at their eagerness, and went on reading. '"May fift. News hath been brought that the plague is broken out in many villages about, but so far we are free, thank God. This day Simeon Wagstaff did come to ask me about the further building I had spoke of to him last summer. I have bid him wait till we know how this sickness shall progress—Mem: To send to Wyesford for more sulphur, since my lady's nostrums be nigh ended. John shall bear a rag well soaked in vinegar to receive the same, and so I trust we shall escape infection.

'"May twentiet. Betty, wife of Owen the cowman, fell sick this day and there is great pother, many swearing that it is the plague. My lady hath departed to see Betty, and will bring me word anon if it be like or no.

'"May twentyfirst. All that aileth Betty, Owen's wife, is a fit of the falling sickness, bad enough, in sooth for her, poor wretch, but no plague. Simeon Wagstaff here this morn to begin my building. I have bid the men uproot what is left of the old elm that fell when I was but a bairn, breaking the window above the stairway."'

'That would be the lost staircase, Sir Ambrose, wouldn't it?' interrupted Lois eagerly.

He nodded. 'Yes; we read, as you may remember, that Sir Stephen meant to give orders to have the broken glass swept up before the bairns should cut themselves playing with it. But this is interesting. I had no notion that it was mentioned here. And I wonder that it has never been spoken of before— Hallo! What's this?'

He had been running his thumb up and down the margin of the page as he spoke, and he detected a certain granular roughness at the edges. He stooped low over the paper, and examined it with the reading-glass.

'Oh, what is it?' gasped Jesanne.

'Bring that lamp over here, Jesanne, will you? Thank you. Now—I wonder—'

Almost breathless with excitement, the pair watched him as he examined the paper narrowly, fingering it carefully with sensitive fingers.

Presently he raised his head. 'Your eyes are younger than mine. Come and look, you two. What do you think?'

They stooped, and peered at the wide margin in silence which was broken by an excited gasp from Jesanne. 'Cousin Ambrose! That's *glue*—or sticky of some kind. It's got worn away, and the page must have been stuck up, and now it's come open. See! There's some on this other page!'

He examined the page closely. 'Yes; you're right, Jesanne. I wonder why that was?'

'Oh, go on reading—go on reading! We're bound to find out then!' implored Lois.

He nodded, and turned back to his careful deciphering of the quaint straggling writing. '"July 1st. This day died Ambrose, third of my Uncle Nick's sons. He bade me mark that Uncle Nick had ever been true to the Faith, even though he cast in his lot with the Parliament, and that he would never have betrayed any of us as Recusants. I bade him be comforted, for that none believed, nor ever did, that tale, save my grandsire, that was so blinded by his anger at my uncle's declaring against the King, that he could see naught of good in his youngest son, but was ready to believe the worst ill against him"—Why, bless me! This is new to me!'

'What does it mean?' asked Jesanne.

'Well, so far as I can see, it means that Sir Ambrose had feared that Nicholas would betray the Chapel to Parliament. You remember that I told you when I showed you the house, Jesanne, that we were Catholic through all the worst of the penal times. No wonder the old man was so bitter if that was what he thought!'

'But who could have stuck it up, then?' asked Lois.

Sir Ambrose turned back to the Journall. 'Let us see if this tells us. Wait patiently, children. I must read to myself first.'

The pair watched him anything but patiently as he read slowly down the great page. At length he looked up. 'It is all here. Caspar wrote down what his grandfather had feared about Nicholas, as his dying cousin had spoken of it. Some years later, just before his own death, apparently, he was re-reading this, and it struck him that to leave such statements on record might bring a slur on the name of Nicholas's family. So he resolved to seal up the two pages very carefully, as, to quote himself: "None can tell if I have wrote aught for those times or no." He must have done his work thoroughly, for I'll vow no one so much as suspected there might be anything written here. Whatever he used to do it—glue, or what not—has perished with the years, no doubt, and so the pages have come apart. And here is something to please you. Listen to this!' And he read out: '"This day the last tale of bricks needed for the work of hiding that which hath bitter memories for some of us was set in place. The House is pinched of some space thereby, but I think it best so. Wind and weather will soon destroy that which, so the old wives say, it would bring ill-luck to raze with mine own hands, and so shall end the worst of the bitterness."' He stopped, and the girls stared at him.

'But what does it mean?' demanded Jesanne at last. 'I don't understand in the least—do you, Lois?'

'Not a word.' Lois shook her curly head.

'What was the thing that bad brought great bitterness to the family but the falling away of Nicholas Gellibrand from the King's cause? And where did old Sir Ambrose first learn of it?'

'*On the staircase!*' Jesanne leaped to the conclusion at once. 'Oh, Cousin Ambrose! Does it mean—'

'I think it means that Caspar walled off the staircase—which must have run up one side of the place—from the *inside*. No doubt he then left the great space that the broken window must have occupied to fall away in ruins. He may even have caused it to be taken down, thus exposing the staircase to the effect of the weather. You can imagine that it would begin to wear away. Ivy and the rest of the creepers that have grown over the walls since the days of Elizabeth would do their share. And then, we must remember two things. First, that the Dragon House was very isolated in those days—far more so than now. And second, that the men working on the estate would all of them be practically illiterate, and therefore would keep no written record of the happening. Probably the family forbade all mention of it, and so memory of it passed away. Girls! It is *outside* the house we must look for the staircase—not inside!'

Chapter XVIII

TOMMY LENDS A PAW

To say that the girls were thrilled at this news is to express it very mildly. When they had fully taken in all that it meant, they were for tearing off at once to hunt round the great house.

'For,' argued Jesanne reasonably, 'stairs made of *stone* couldn't possibly rot away altogether. It isn't as if they were of wood, is it? There must be something there, even after all these centuries.'

Sir Ambrose quite agreed with her statement, but he flatly refused to permit any wandering round the house after dark on a misty February evening.

'No; wait for the morning. I will send word to Miss Mercier that we shall not need her after eleven,' he said. 'You may do lessons till then. After that, if it is fine, we will make the rounds outside and see if we can possibly find any traces. Though I warn you,' he added, 'that if there are any, they must be quite slight, or they would have been found years ago by some of the men who clip the creepers every year. Indeed, I can't understand how it is that they have never been noticed. And yet they haven't, or we should have heard of them before this.'

'Perhaps what you said about the family forbidding any talk of it may have been handed down among the estate families,' suggested Lois. 'Their descendants still live on the estate, don't they?'

He nodded thoughtfully. 'That's a good idea, Lois. I shouldn't be surprised if you were right. Probably old gaffers repeated the prohibition to their sons, who handed it on to *their* sons. In the course of time, no doubt, the reason for it was forgotten; but not the ban itself. I must make inquiries presently, and find out.'

And, to cut a long story short, this proved to have been exactly what had happened. One very old man, not far from his century, could remember, when he was a lad of sixteen, being employed to clip the creepers which clothed the Dragon House, and his father had told him that at one part there were the remains of stone steps, but he must never speak of them, for it was forbidden, and he would most likely be turned away if he ever mentioned it. As his own family had consisted of daughters, it had never occurred to him to repeat the warning, and so it had been completely forgotten until the arrival of Jesanne, and her determination to find the lost staircase had started all the interest.

In the meantime, the two girls proclaimed aloud their grievance at having to wait for the infra-red-rays photograph of the two pages still stuck together, and only ceased when Sir Ambrose suggested that they still had half an hour before Lois's uncle would arrive to take her home, and the best way of employing the time would be going through the Journall to see if they could find any more.

It was very thrilling, and over and over again one or another cried out that *this* page felt thicker than the rest. But when they tested it with the lights, they could find nothing to make it seem possible that it was more than one page; and, as Sir Ambrose had to keep reminding them, there were often flaws in the rag-made paper of the time, and pages of a heavier texture might be expected here and there.

Mr Jennings arrived to find them hard at it, and had to have the whole story told him. He was quite as excited as any of them, for, naturally, he knew of the story of the lost staircase, since his own family had lived for so many generations on the estate. It was past eight o'clock when at length he succeeded in remembering that Lois should have been at home half an hour ago, and the Dragon House dinner must be spoiling. He prised her away from the Journall, and bore her off, partly solaced by a promise that nothing should be done about hunting outside until she was there.

Then Jesanne and Sir Ambrose went in to dinner, to be waited on by a somewhat injured Totton, who knew that the entrée was spoiled by the delay.

Lessons were something of a farce next morning. Miss Mercier had real cause for indignation at the lack of interest shown by her pupils. She became her old self, and assured them that unless they showed a great improvement during the last hour she would speak to Sir Ambrose about their inattention and bad behaviour, and ask that they might have lessons in the afternoon.

The pair knew that if she did, Sir Ambrose was quite likely to back her up, for they were well aware that they could plead no excuse to which he was likely to listen. So they made a big effort, and controlled their rising excitement, and for the remaining hour the governess found her task much easier.

Eleven o'clock came at long last, and the excited couple were all for rushing off at once. But *that*, Miss Mercier would not permit. They must take their cocoa and biscuits before they went, and they must sit down, and have them properly, like young gentlewomen. And Agnes brought a message from Sir Ambrose to the effect that he was detained by an unexpected visitor, and would not be ready for them for another half-hour.

'Oh, *bother*!' grumbled Jesanne. 'Why on earth do visitors come in the morning? Nobody wants them—the afternoon is the proper time for visiting.'

'Please don't talk nonsense, Jesanne!' said Miss Mercier coldly. 'You are too big to behave in this babyish fashion. Come and sit down and drink your cocoa before it is quite cold. There will be plenty of time for whatever it is you are going to do after half-past eleven.'

Jesanne sat down—they were in her own sitting-room where they always had their 'elevenses'—and did as she was told somewhat sulkily. But Little Tommy and Sanchia got most of her biscuits when Miss Mercier was not looking.

Half-way through the waiting period, Agnes came to say that the governess was wanted on the telephone, so she left the girls to themselves for a few minutes. As she said later, somewhat tearfully, no one could expect that anything would happen in that short period.

Left alone, the pair strayed over to one of the windows which was wide open, for the day was fine and very mild, with more than a hint of spring in the air. They hung out, looking down at the ivy-clad wall beneath them, wondering if this was 'the staircase wall,' as Lois called it.

The other window was open too, and someone else was moved to an adventure of his own. Unheeded by his mistress, Little Tommy, who had been sitting on the sill, as good as gold, suddenly took it into his head to make an expedition. He began climbing down by the ivy, which at this point was of three centuries' growth, and almost strong enough to take the weight of a man. He frisked gaily off, followed by the wistful gaze of Sanchia, who had enough sense to know that she could not follow.

At first, all went well. The adventurous kitten clambered down, intent on business of his own. Then, how it happened no one could ever say. However it might be, Tommy slipped, and fell through the ivy, landing in a queer, damp place, from which there seemed to be no outlet. He tried to climb up again, but in vain. It was dark, and very cold and miserable. Tommy was a pampered young thing, and he didn't like it. He set up a despairing yowl, for, in falling, he had contrived to bruise a paw, and his climbing efforts had made matters worse.

Jesanne and Lois, at the window in the other wall, heard the squall and also the wild whimperings of Sanchia, who knew that her small chum was in trouble, and was capering about on the window-seat, looking anxiously downward to see if she could find a means of going to the rescue.

The two girls at once guessed what had happened.

'Oh, Tommy's tried to get down by the ivy and fallen and hurt himself!' cried Jesanne, rushing to the other window, and pushing Sanchia away so that she might lean out. 'Tommy—Tommy!'

At the sound of her voice, Tommy uttered a fearful cry which left his mistress under the impression that he was being tortured. 'He's caught in the ivy somewhere!' she cried. And before Lois could stop her, she had swung herself across the sill, and was climbing down the ivy in the direction of the shrieks which ascended.

There should have been no real danger. As I have said, the ivy was tremendously strong and thick here, and quite capable of supporting a much greater weight than Jesanne's. She herself was well accustomed to climbing, and had a good head for heights. Lois had the sense to keep quiet, though she hung out of the window, watching her friend with, so she said later, her heart in her mouth.

Down and down went Jesanne, swinging from branch to branch with the agility of a monkey. Little Tommy was still informing the universe of his woes, and she found it easy enough to find out just where he was. She reached the place in safety, though she still could not see the wicked kitten, who even yet yelled heartrendingly.

'Oh, be quiet!' she cried. 'I'm just above you, somewhere. I'll get you out in a moment.'

Clinging with both feet and one hand, she tried to part the thick ivy with the other. She thought that there must be some niche here into which her kitten had fallen, though she wondered that he had been unable to extricate himself. At length she contrived to peer through, and was rewarded by seeing two uncanny green lamps shining in the darkness.

'There you are, you nuisance!' she ejaculated. 'And how I'm to haul you out of that is more than I can tell. The ivy's so thick here.'

'Be careful, Jesanne!' called Lois from overhead. 'Can you stick there while I rush round to the stables and get the men to bring the ladders?'

'Yes; but be quick,' called back Jesanne. 'This isn't awfully comfy.'

Lois tore off by the back-stairs, and caused consternation in the stables by bursting into the yard, gasping out, 'Fetch the ladders! Miss Jesanne's stuck on the ivy up the wall!'

At once all was bustle and scurry. Two of the men hurried to bring the long ladders used for the spring clipping, while two more, seizing horse-blankets, rushed off to the terrace, led by Lois, ready to catch Jesanne if she should slip.

As they tore past the library window, Sir Ambrose saw them. Instinctively, he guessed that something was wrong, and, with barely a word to the Rector (who happened to be his visitor), he seized his crutches, and swung himself out into the great hall at an amazing rate.

Miss Mercier was just leaving the telephone-room, a little ante-room off the hall, and realised that there was trouble. Her employer's face told that. And here was the Rector, hurrying after him. She relinquished her intention of running upstairs to the girls, and followed them on to the terrace.

By this time, half the household had been roused, and were hastening to the scene of the trouble. Some of the men, at work in the grounds, were coming too; the head-gardener, with the aid of an under-gardener, carrying one of the ladders used during apple-picking time.

There was a little crowd on the terrace by the time the governess got to the place where they were looking up at Jesanne, who clung like a monkey, while Little Tommy's squalls would certainly have brought an R.S.P.C.A. inspector on the scene in double-quick time if he had been anywhere within hearing.

Miss Mercier's first feeling was one of outrage that any pupil of hers should be caught by the household in such an undignified scrape. The others had managed to control themselves, and do nothing to startle the girl. The governess, already irritated and upset by the tiresomeness of the pair at lessons, lost her head.

'Jesanne! You naughty, troublesome child!' she cried. 'How dare you do such a thing? Come down at once!'

Jesanne always said that she couldn't be sure what happened. Whether it was the suddenness of Miss Mercier's denunciation, or whether it was the truly awful howl Little Tommy set up just then, or whether it was that some new marvellous idea popped into her head, and brought about a momentary unguarded movement, she never could tell. However it was, foot and hand suddenly slipped. One foot went right through the ivy, and touched—*nothing*! Even in that horrible moment she felt a triumphant thrill go through her, for this was proof positive that her thought had been right, and she was actually standing outside the remains of the Lost Staircase, while Little Tommy must be *sitting* on it. Then she had lost her grip, and was falling down—down—down!

She heard a chorus of shrieks, above which Lois's agonised yell was clearly distinct. She shrieked herself in the horrid shock of the fall. Then she had landed into something which gave, and suddenly tore—she could hear the sounds of rending—under the sudden impact of her weight, and she crashed—mercifully, only by a few feet—on to the stone flags of the terrace. There was a stunning bang. Stars and flashing lights danced before her eyes. Then darkness came, and overwhelmed her completely.

Chapter XIX

THE STAIRCASE IS FOUND!

LOIS was the first to spring forward. Sir Ambrose was too unsteady on his crutches for any such sudden movement; but the lithe schoolgirl leapt to the little heap on the terrace, and dropped on her knees by its side.

'*Jesanne!*' she cried. Then: 'Totton, go and ring up the doctor! Someone fetch rugs to cover her—*quickly*!'

'Take a door off its hinges for a litter!' exclaimed Miss Mercier.

Sir Ambrose, who was standing beside them now, grief and horror in his face as he looked down on the last heir to the Dragon House, negatived this firmly. 'Certainly not! No one must touch her till the doctor comes. Hiles, bring that horse-blanket here. Now, Lois, do you think you can get it over her?—Gently, child. There; that's better.'

A more heartrending miaowing than before made him lift his head with a jerk. 'Get those ladders against the wall and fetch that kitten down, someone. Miss Jesanne will be sure to ask about him as soon as she recovers consciousness.' His voice shook on the last word; for who could say if Jesanne would ever recover consciousness in this world?

Totton came back along the terrace, blank dismay on his face.

'Well?' said his master abruptly.

'The doctor's out, sir—gone to Gwyn-y-ffrioch, and not likely to be back for some hours. I sent Owens there to bring him.'

'How?' demanded Sir Ambrose. 'If he takes his motor-cycle, he'll have to walk the best part of the way up the hillside.'

'Owens remembered that, sir. He has taken Taffy. He went off bareback, for I saw him, riding like the dev—I beg pardon, sir!'

Sir Ambrose nodded abstractedly. Then he turned round to Miss Mercier. 'Miss Mercier! I want you to send a cable at once for me. Get on to the post-office at Wyesford, and tell them it's urgent.' He took out his ivory tablets, and scribbled a brief message down before handing them to the governess. 'There! Ask them to get it off at once. Here's the address— *What's that?*'

'That' was the purring of a car up the drive. Even as the frightened cluster turned, it stopped, the door opened, and the doctor himself leapt out, grabbing his bag, and came racing across the lawns, up the grassy bank, and over the balustrade at a speed which landed him among them almost before they had realised who it was. With no waste of words, he knelt down beside the still little form under the horse-blanket. For the next minute there was a breathless silence as he made a hasty examination.

'She's alive,' he said at length. 'But we must get her away from here. Where is the nearest room?'

'The library,' said Sir Ambrose, speaking quickly. 'Lois, run and clear the settee. Spike, fetch blankets. Two of you men get a door off its hinges for a stretcher.'

Everyone hastened to do his bidding. And when the door was brought, Jesanne was lifted on to it very tenderly and carefully, and then borne into the house, and taken to the library, where Lois had cleared not only the settee, but the great table which stood under the window. Seeing this, the doctor motioned to the men to lay the improvised stretcher on it, and then sent them all away except Sir Ambrose, Lois, and Spike, while he made his examination. Jesanne moaned a little as he touched her, but the heavy black lashes never lifted from the white cheeks.

It seemed hours to the anxious watchers while he cut away her clothes, aided by Spike, and then examined her. But at length he turned back, drawing a blanket over her before he did so.

'A twisted ankle, sundry bruises, and a fracture of the left wrist,' he said. 'She must have struck her head, too, and there is concussion—but only slight. How far did she fall?'

'From the ivy, half-way up to her sitting-room window. But really, I think she only banged herself when the blanket gave,' said Lois quickly.

'How far was that?'

'About so.' Lois held her hand up to her own waistline, and looked dubiously at Sir Ambrose. 'I'm sure it wasn't more, for the men were holding it. It tore when she fell into it, and that's how she landed on the flags.'

The doctor nodded. 'I see. Well, thank God for that. Unless she managed to twist herself at all, I don't think there can be any internal injury, which was what I feared. However, we shall know better, when she recovers consciousness. Meanwhile, I'll set the wrist and bandage the ankle, and then we'll get her to bed. It'll mean a few weeks there, but nothing to matter, Sir Ambrose. Mrs Spike, will you get me some hot water? Lois, bring my bag here, and then go and send me someone with a little common sense, please.'

They scattered to do his bidding, and Lois, evading Miss Mercier, who had finished her telephoning and was coming to ask how Jesanne was, called Cook to the doctor's aid, and then hunted for Agnes, whom she sent to open Jesanne's bed and fill hot-water bottles. After that, she made her way back to the library, to be caught at the foot of the stairs by the governess, who clutched her arm tightly.

'Where are you going, Lois? Why did you not stop when I called you before? You might have known how anxious I would be.'

Now, Lois blamed Miss Mercier for the final catastrophe. She always maintained that if the governess had not called out, Jesanne would not have lost her hold and fallen. Therefore she was by no means disposed to relieve Miss Mercier's anxiety. So all she said was, 'I am going back to the library to see if I am wanted for any more errands. I couldn't stop because the doctor had sent me on a message, and I had to go at once. Please let me go; they may need me.'

'Tell me how Jesanne is?' commanded Miss Mercier imperiously.

'She's still unconscious,' replied Lois.

'Is she badly hurt?' Miss Mercier's voice actually trembled as she put the question. An older person would have seen how she was suffering, and eased her mind.

But not Lois! 'She *deserves* a fright!' thought that young lady. 'If she hadn't yelled, nothing would have happened, 'cos the ladders would have got there in plenty of time.' So she merely shook her head, and replied, 'She's twisted her ankle, and fractured a wrist, and she has concussion. The doctor can't say if she's hurt inside or not until later. May I go now, please?'

Miss Mercier released her mechanically, and Lois shot off down the passage leading from the great hall to the library, only to be turned back at the door by Sir Ambrose, who ordered her to 'run away at once!'

Lois had the sense to do as she was told, but she had no mind to be captured again by her governess; so she slipped into Sir Ambrose's office, got out to the terrace through the window, and thus contrived to run round the house and gain the telephone-room without encountering poor Miss Mercier, who, thanks to her naughty pupil's unkindness, had to wait in an agony of fear until one of the elders was free to come and relieve her mind.

Meanwhile, Jesanne, with ankle bandaged and wrist properly

set, and her numerous bruises anointed with a special lotion of the doctor's own concoction, was lifted on her improvised stretcher and borne carefully up the wide, shallow stairs, and along to the pretty bedroom, where Agnes was waiting, the bed opened, hot-water bottles before the fire, ready filled, and additional pillows on a near-by chair in readiness.

Sir Ambrose was not too much upset to cast her a grateful glance, though he waited till later to thank her. Jesanne was gently eased off the stretcher on to the bed, where Mrs Spike, helped by the doctor, contrived to get a nightdress on her. Then the curtains were drawn, darkening the room, and the housekeeper sat down to keep vigilant watch on the young mistress till she should come to herself.

'It won't be long, though,' said the doctor, drawing on his driving-gloves in the hall. 'She's had a nasty knock, and she won't be able to wear a hat for the next two or three weeks. I expect she'll be very sore, and sorry for herself, when she does come round; but, so far as I can judge, there's nothing that a few weeks won't cure. Keep her quiet; only drinks until I see her again—no food, mind!—and I don't think you need worry. And now, Sir Ambrose, I'm going to recommend bed for you for the rest of the day. You've had a bad shock, and you're not too fit yet. Don't you worry about that young monkey of yours. She'll live to give you more shocks than this. I'll look in about six this evening, when I expect she'll be rousing. Now get off to bed, and try and get a nap.'

'You're sure she hasn't injured her spine in any way?' asked Sir Ambrose, his voice shaking a little. 'I dread that more than anything. After Peter—' His voice trailed off into silence, and the doctor reassured him at once.

'She fell on her side. There's not a mark on her back, though the left side will be black and blue tomorrow, I'm afraid. It's a wonder she didn't dislocate her collar-bone! Well, they say there's a special Providence watching over fools and children, and there's no doubt about it, He had an eye on Jesanne this morning. It was lucky, though, that I got here so soon—I met your man Owens on the way. My word for it, Sir Ambrose, there's nothing badly wrong with her. You go and get that nap. You're in almost worse case than she is.'

His mind relieved, Sir Ambrose obeyed the doctor, and when Lois came back from the kitchen, where she had taken refuge from Miss Mercier, he had gone to bed.

'You'd better go home,' said the Rector, who had been collecting the papers through which he and Sir Ambrose had been looking when the accident happened. 'Go and get your hat and coat, and I'll run you round and explain things to your aunt. You can cycle over this evening to inquire after Jesanne. But there's nothing for you to do here. She has to be kept very quiet for the next few days, so they won't allow you to see her. I don't suppose you feel much like lessons, and I doubt if Miss Mercier does. Poor soul! I hope someone has told her there's nothing seriously wrong.'

'Well, *I* didn't!' said Lois defiantly. 'It was her fault it happened. I wasn't going to say anything.'

The Rector turned on her with a look that brought the colour to her face in a rush.

'You nasty, spiteful little *baby*!' he said calmly. 'You ought to be ashamed of yourself!'

'Well, I'm not,' muttered Lois resentfully.

What would have happened, it is hard to tell, but just then one of the men came in, bearing an equally resentful and very sooty kitten, who snarled and spat at his rescuer most ungratefully.

Lois ran forward and caught the real cause of all the trouble to her, plentifully besmearing her clean blouse as she did so. 'Poor little man!' she said. 'Come along to the kitchen and Lois will give you some hot milk.' Then she turned and raced off with Little Tommy, who still regarded it as a hard world, and swore at her the whole way.

Meanwhile, the man had turned to the Rector in some excitement. 'Excuse me, sir, but could you tell me where Sir Ambrose is?'

'The doctor sent him to bed,' replied the Rector, packing his papers into his despatch-case.

The man's face fell. 'When do you think I could see him, sir?'

'Well, not before evening—if then. Is there anything wrong?' The Rector finished off sharply, for he felt anxious about the old man.

'Oh, no, sir—not to say *wrong*. Only I thought he'd like to know that there's *steps* there where the cat fell through. We had to cut some of the ivy right away, and he was sittin' on one of 'em. None on us can make it out, and I thought Sir Ambrose ought to know, like.'

The Rector raised his eyebrows. 'Steps? Are you sure, Powell?'

'Certain sure, sir. You come and see for yourself. The ladders is still up agen the wall.'

But the chiming of the clock prevented any researches for the moment. With an exclamation, the Rector shut the catch of his case and hunted round for his hat. 'I must go at once. I have a meeting in Wyesford at two o'clock. But I'll be back by five, and I'll see into it then. Don't disturb Sir Ambrose, Powell. I hope he is asleep. We must remember that he is an old man, and this morning's shock has been bad for him.'

'Very good, sir. You know best, o' course.' Powell began to move away. Then he came back. 'Beg pardon, sir. Sir Ambrose ain't bad, is he?'

'Oh, no. But he's had a nasty shock. However, I expect a few hours' rest will put him right again. Meantime, don't gossip about your find, and warn the others to keep still tongues. Better move the ladders for the present. You can get them when I come back at five. I'll see your discovery then. Now I must see Miss Mercier, and set her mind at rest, and then I must run.'

And with this the good-hearted Rector went off, first to seek the nearly frantic governess, and reassure her about Jesanne, and then to get into his little runabout and risk a summons for driving to the danger of the general public in his haste to get back for his lunch before he must set off for Wyesford.

Chapter XX

EVERYTHING COMES RIGHT

'THEN I *was* right, and it *was* the staircase?' Jesanne spoke with rather more excitement than the doctor would have thought good for her, even though it was a fortnight later, and she was sitting up in a big chair in her sitting-room, well propped with pillows, for her bruises still ached. Her foot was on a stool, and her wrist in a sling. Mercifully, the fracture had proved to be a mere fracture and not a break, and she was healing as well as every healthy child does. She had suffered badly for a day or two, between an outsize in headaches, the aching of her hurts, and—as soon as she could think of it—unsatisfied curiosity. But now she was up, and Lois had been allowed to come and sit with her for an hour.

Lois nodded in reply to the question. 'Yes; though how you could manage to think of it when you were falling like that is more than I can imagine! Powell had to cut away whole chunks of the ivy before he could get at Little Tommy, and he found the steps—parts of them, anyhow. The Rector went up that evening when he came back from Wyesford, and he said it was quite true. Then Sir Ambrose was told, and he made them cut away the ivy right down. You can see it splendidly now.'

'And I'm stuck in this chair and can't move! It's too sickening for words! What's it like, Lois?'

'Oh, very ruiny, of course. Whole pieces are missing. But they're *there* all right, and Sir Ambrose says it's thanks to you they've been found. He was very thrilled about it.'

'Thanks to Little Tommy, *I* should say,' laughed Jesanne,

recovering from her momentary annoyance at being out of all the excitement. 'If he hadn't fallen, we might never have found them, for Cousin Ambrose says that the bottom ones are quite gone.'

'That's nonsense! If we hadn't found them low down, they'd have used the ladders, and they'd have been found sooner or later.'

'Well, I hope the doctor lets me move about soon, for I'm simply aching to see them. Isn't it a thrill! After all these years to have found them! Has the photo been taken yet, by the way?'

'Not yet. Sir Ambrose says he's waiting till you're fit again so that you're in *some* of it, anyway.'

'Isn't he a dear!' sighed Jesanne happily. 'He says he's got a gorgeous surprise coming for me presently, and I've got to hurry up and get well for it. He needn't worry about that part! I *hate* being tied up here!'

Sir Ambrose himself came in at that moment, and the two girls promptly beset him with questions about when the photograph would be taken.

'Some time next week, I expect,' he said. 'You must wait till then. And now, Lois, I'm going to turn you out. You've had an hour and a half with Jesanne, and the idea was only an hour at first. You can come over to see her tomorrow at the same time, and by next week I expect she'll be walking about with a stick. Her ankle seems to be coming on nicely.'

Lois got up reluctantly. 'I hate to go. It's seemed such a long time without you, Jesanne. And I do hate having lessons by myself.'

'It won't hurt you,' said Sir Ambrose hard-heartedly. 'It's no more than you deserve after the way you treated poor Miss Mercier.'

Lois looked unconvinced. She maintained that the governess had been to blame for Jesanne's accident, and nothing could make her change her mind. However, Sir Ambrose was holding the door open for her, so she could only say goodbye to her chum and go home, since this was Saturday and, therefore, a holiday.

The next excitement was the photographing of the glued pages, and of sundry others about which Sir Ambrose was doubtful. When the prints came, however, they found that only the first had been fastened. The rest owed their extra thickness to faults in the paper. But what was written on those two pages was surprise enough for anything. Jesanne was downstairs by that time, able to walk without her stick, though her wrist was still in the sling. Her bruises were almost gone, and her cheeks were beginning to grow pink again.

The big envelope had been brought by the Professor himself, and Sir Ambrose had summoned the two girls from the schoolroom to see the results of the photography.

Very excitedly they bent over it, and slowly deciphered the writing which had been hidden all these years.

'"October tenth. This daie came home my brother Nick from some secret journey, and told mee that alle was wel. He hath never left the Faith tho how hee kept it hid from Cromwell and his men hee wil notte saie. Howbeit, my sire was rongge when hee did bid Brother Nick leeve the howse, for that hee was traytor to his kynge, and woud be traietor to his Faith. Nick telleth mee thatte hee hath hidde all papers in the old cracke on the grate stair where wee hid thinges when we were bairns. They wille bee safe there, for none is like to kno of thee plaice save ouselves. Soe, if General Cromwel send fifty men to seek, they will come by nort of proffitte to him or eny."'

'Whatever could they have been?' interrupted Jesanne.

'I have no idea,' replied her cousin. 'Possibly lists of other recusants and the fugitive priests who visited them at long intervals when it was thought safe.'

'But—but—but,' stammered Lois in wild excitement,

'won't those papers be there *yet*? Surely if they had fallen out before someone would have found them? But no one has said anything about them, so they must still be hidden where Nicholas Gellibrand hid them!'

Sir Ambrose started. 'Bless me, Lois, I never thought of that. We must have those stairs seen to as soon as possible. Such lists would be of deep interest to many. And there may be even more important papers among them.'

'Oh, let's go and find them *now*!' implored Jesanne.

'In this weather?' He looked at the window, which was lashed by sheets of driving rain, and smiled. 'Oh, no, Jesanne. They've waited so long they may well wait a little longer. Let us go on with this now, and if it's fine tomorrow, I'll have the ladders set up, and send the men up to see if they can find any cracks or hidey-holes.'

'It ought to be *us* to go up,' murmured Jesanne discontentedly.

'Not until that wrist of yours is right again. We'll wait for that if you like.' But he smiled to himself as he said it, for well he knew that the impatient pair would never consent to that.

He was quite right. They agreed that the men should be sent up on the morrow if the weather were fine; and meantime they contented themselves with continuing with their reading, while the Professor, who was an old acquaintance of Miss Mercier's, renewed his friendship with that lady in Jesanne's sitting-room.

'"November twentiet. I have myselfe covered up the crack with plaster to make alle saife."'

'Stephen's spelling is literally *wild*!' interjected Lois at this point.

'Oh, he spells as well as most country squires of his time,' replied Sir Ambrose tolerantly. 'Shall we go on?'

"Yes, please. I didn't mean to interrupt.'

Sir Ambrose resumed his reading. '"There have beene meny

men hereabowts, and tis saide that Wee bee notte saife from Parlement, wych sendeth up agenst Wyesford. Yett doe I thinke thatte wee bee so farre from thee rode that wee shalle scape. And soe I hope."'

'And they did, of course,' interrupted Jesanne.

'Oh, yes; the Dragon House escaped, though Wyesford fell, and the Parliamentary troops stabled their horses in the Cathedral.'

'How *horrid* of them!' Lois lifted a flushed face. 'Why, the Cathedral is God's House. I wonder that they *dared*!'

'Oh, they did worse than that. The windows went, of course. And a good many of the old effigies were destroyed. However, that is all gone and past, so we won't trouble about it now. Instead we'll go on with our reading.'

Lois calmed down and he continued. The pages were full of interest to the three who pored over them. Stephen's spelling was, as Lois had said, wild in the extreme, and some words had to be guessed at from their context. Still, they were able to make very fair sense of it all.

They learned that Nicholas had indeed hidden papers of great value in the aforesaid crack in the stairs; for not only were there the lists of 'recusants' of the neighbourhood, and those priests who might visit them; but there was also a plan of the Dragon House, showing where the secret chapel and the priest's hole were, and if those had fallen into enemy hands it would have meant the death or imprisonment of a good many people, to say nothing of what might have befallen the Gellibrands.

Besides this, there were stated to be a rosary, reliquary, and 'the little statew of thee Blest Vergin wych my greatgrandsire browt with him from Florence when hee was theyre.'

Then followed two lines of which no one could make any sense, though they all tried. Stephen Gellibrand must have written the last of his entry at great speed, and the writing, never very good at the best of times, became positively unreadable just here. The last two sentences were fairly distinct, however.

'Word is browt mee that theyre be Parlement men a-coming and I must hasten to finish this and hyde itte with alle that is left us of valew in the preest's hole for saifety.'

Here, the pages ended; and the two Gellibrands and Lois were left to ponder on what they had read.

'What does he mean by "alle that is left us of valew"?' demanded Jesanne at last.

'Gellibrands had melted down much of their plate, and sent the results to the royal funds,' explained Sir Ambrose. 'That is why we have so little belonging to that period and before. Most of our plate dates from the reign of Charles II and later. I believe Sir Paul Gellibrand added largely to it, for we have a fine Georgian collection. Well, that is the story. What happened afterwards we can only guess, for Stephen hasn't thought fit to say in his next entry.' He turned to the Journall, and found the page. 'See; it was written about two months later, and there is no mention of Parliamentary troops coming. Something must have turned them aside, for it is certain that the Dragon House never had to offer hospitality to those gentry. *What*, we can't tell. We can only guess.'

'Well, as long as they didn't come,' said Lois comfortably. 'If they had, they might have done endless damage. If they could smash up the Cathedral as they did, they'd probably have tried to finish off the wood-carving.'

'It is possible. Some of the fanatics thought it wrong to have carving or pictures of any kind, for they called it "breaking the second commandment."'

'How awful!' said Jesanne.

'Oh, it was only the fanatics. But, of course, we can't tell whether any such were included in the troop that were sent this way. I wonder what hindered them coming?' mused Sir Ambrose.

However, that question was not to be answered just then. Totton came to say that tea was ready in the hall, so they put away the Journall and the photographs, and went to enjoy a meal which caused the Head of the Dragon House to declare that falling from the ivy had given Jesanne an extra appetite. And after tea the Rector appeared to make a call, and when he went it was time for dinner.

'Never mind! The men will find that crack tomorrow, and we'll get the lists and things, and that'll be so much,' Jesanne comforted Lois, who was wild with curiosity as to what had happened.

'There might be something there to tell us what happened,' said Lois more cheerfully.

'So there might! I hadn't thought of that. We'll ask Cousin Ambrose what he thinks about it at dinner. Hurry up, Lois! I'm ready, and you still haven't put on your frock.'

'Agnes dressed you,' retorted Lois with a grimace.—'All right, Agnes. I shan't be a minute now.' She pulled on her frock, saw that her hair was tidy, and then followed her chum along the corridor and down the stairs to the dining-room, where they found Sir Ambrose waiting for them patiently, and Totton looking reproachful, since they were five minutes late already.

Chapter XXI

THE LAST MYSTERIES SOLVED

ON the morrow the men reared ladders against the side of the house, while the girls and Sir Ambrose hung out of Jesanne's sitting-room window, ready to learn anything from the search. The ivy had all been torn down here, and the remains of the old stone staircase were clearly visible. They seemed to have been narrow stairs, rather steep in pitch, and, towards the foot, they had completely vanished. What was left was green with the drippings of centuries, as well as moss and lichens. They came as far as the end wall of the corridor, where they had probably finished in early days. It would be a matter of some difficulty to find the crack where Nicholas Gellibrand had hidden the all-important papers, and Sir Ambrose rather doubted that it would be found. It might have been towards the base of the stairway, in which case the papers at least must have been destroyed.

Jesanne and Lois refused to believe this for one moment.

'If the papers had gone, the other things must have been found,' argued Jesanne. 'It doesn't say what the statue was made of, but it couldn't have gone to pieces so soon, and there isn't a word in the Journall about it.'

'No: that's true. But it might have been found by someone who either destroyed it or else hid it and sold it,' argued Sir Ambrose. 'Some of those statues were valuable, set with gems and made of gold or silver. If it were found by a dishonest person, he had every incentive to keep quiet about his find.'

'Well, I expect the crack was pretty high up, anyhow,' said Lois.

'We'll hope so. But I don't want you two to build on it, and then be badly disappointed.'

'We shan't be,' declared Jesanne stoutly, as she squirmed herself into a more comfortable position, with Sanchia cuddled down beside her, and Little Tommy on her lap.

He laughed, but said no more. Instead, the three watched the men—Silas Hiles the gardener, and Jones and Morgan the under-gardeners—with almost breathless interest.

At first nothing came to light. Step after step was tried; but though there were plenty of cracks, none yielded anything of more interest than a Queen Anne shilling, which Morgan found in a niche between two stairs, and a pair of small embroidery scissors, all rusted, which Sir Ambrose vowed he recognised as a pair he had thrown out of the window in a fit of bad temper one day when he was a small boy.

He handled them gently. 'They were my mother's, and she had refused to let me go to the May Fair in Wyesford,' he told the two girls. 'There was a lot of illness about at the time, and she forbade it. I had a fine temper of my own in those days, and I can remember snatching up the scissors from her little embroidery table and flinging them out of the window in my rage. They must have caught in the ivy and slipped through, for I remember they were never found, though I hunted all over when I had recovered. They were favourites of hers, and she was very much distressed. Though,' he added, 'she was more distressed because my father came in at that moment and gave me the whipping I certainly deserved. I am glad to have them as a memento of her.' And he put them very carefully into his watch-pocket.

The girls looked at him sympathetically. They knew that his mother had died when he was a boy of fifteen, and that he had been almost inconsolable at her death. They were silent for a few minutes. Then a call from Jones brought their heads out of the window again.

'There's summat 'ere, Sir Ambrose,' called the man.

'Oh, what is it—what is it?' cried Jesanne, wriggling with excitement.

'Tell yer in a minute, Miss Jesanne.—Lever that stone a bit, Jim, and I'll get it out.'

Eagerly they watched them while the stone, which was loose, but heavy, was cautiously levered up by Morgan. Then Jones slipped his hand in the crack, and presently pulled out—a glove!

But what a glove! It was gauntleted, with wonderful embroidery on the gauntlet and the backs in what had been gold thread, though only a stitch or two, rotted and black, remained of it. Two or three tiny seed-pearls were still held in place among the stitchery, and, in its day, it must have been a thing of beauty.

'How tiny!' commented Lois, as she tried to slip a slim paw into it regardless of any insects that might have made their home in it. 'I suppose it must have belonged to one of the Gellibrand children, Sir Ambrose?'

He shook his head as he took it from her. 'No; it's a lady's glove. They had small hands in those days, remember. What size gloves do you take, Lois?'

'Six-and-a-half. But that's only for length.' And Lois spread out a slender, long-fingered hand.

'I should think this was a five. Ladies had small hands in those days: they didn't play tennis and golf and hockey, nor do the thousand and one things you modern girls do to stretch yours. I don't suppose any child ever wore such an elaborate affair. This is a lady's riding-glove—probably dating from the seventeen hundreds, though I can't be sure about that.—Well, Jones; is there anything else there?'

'Can't feel anything else, sir. I'll go on to the next step, shall I?'

'Yes. Mind how you let that stone down, Morgan. We don't want any accidents.'

'I'll be careful, sir,' replied Morgan, as Jones scrambled out of the way. 'Oopsy-daisy! There she goes!'

Nothing was found on the next step, nor the next, nor the next, and there remained only five steps to explore. Lois and Jesanne were watching impatiently. It would be too bad if, after all, the cache had been made at the bottom of the stairs, and everything had vanished.

Hiles, who was going ahead of the two younger men, was on the ladder, just above the third step from the top. He had found a fairly large crack, quite big enough for him to slip a hand in, and the children followed him with eager eyes.

For a few moments he felt about. Then he looked up at the group at the window. 'Summat 'ere, sir,' he called. 'I can't just get a hold of it, though. Here, Morgan, you've smaller 'ands nor me. Come you up an' try.'

He went on up the ladder, and Morgan, a young fellow with long, thin hands, took his place, and felt in the cranny. He was able to push in further than Hiles, who was sturdily built, with big, gnarled hands and thick wrists. 'It's a-comin', sir!' he called. 'Summat round it is—most like a ball!'

He drew his hand carefully back, and in it was a round thing, black and shiny where the late February sun caught it. He climbed up the ladder to the window, and handed it to his master. Sir Ambrose took it carefully, and the girls crowded round to see the object, Jesanne tumbling Little Tommy most unceremoniously off her lap to do so.

'What is it?' she asked breathlessly. 'A ball—someone's ball from *those* times?'

'It's too small,' objected Lois.

'And it's the wrong stuff,' added Sir Ambrose. 'I don't imagine that anyone ever gave a child a *silver* ball to play with.'

'*Silver!*' Both girls echoed.

'Silver—and see here.' He gave it a quick, deft twist, and half of it came away.

'A box—a little box!' cried Jesanne. 'Oh—and with holes in it, too—see!'

She pointed to the tiny holes which were visible on this cleaner side, but not to be seen with a cursory glance on the outside.

'A pouncet box,' pronounced Sir Ambrose—'late Charles II, I think. Lois, run and call Agnes. We'll get her to clean it up, and then we shall see it better. Is there anything else, Morgan?'

'Don't know, sir. Shall I try again?'

'Yes; where one thing may be, there may be another.'

Morgan went down the ladder again, while Lois flew to fetch Agnes and the silver-polishing things at top speed. She didn't want to lose any of the fun.

Morgan was rooting round in the hole when she came back, and Jones had brought his lever, and was levering up the top of the step very carefully, while Hiles felt along the last step of all to see if he could find any crack.

Suddenly, Morgan withdrew his hand, and held up a little leather bag.

'Oh, is it *it*?' cried Lois.

'Nonsense, Lois. That would never hold anything like what we are looking for. This is probably someone's savings. Let me see, Morgan.'

Morgan brought the little bag, and stood on the rung of the ladder as keen as anyone to know what he had found.

The bag was tied with strings which were knotted tightly together. But the string had perished during the long years the thing had lain in its hidey-hole, and came away, bringing part of the leather with them.

At once there poured out a perfect rain of small, round things, one of which hit Jones, who uttered a yell. They fell to the terrace below, Sir Ambrose only saving the last two or three with an effort.

He turned them out into the palm of his hand, which he held out for those interested to see.

'*Marbles!*' cried Jesanne with a peal of laughter. 'Oh, they're marbles! And I thought they'd be pearls and diamonds at the very least!'

Marbles they were—made of some kind of stone, and, when you came to look at them, very roughly finished. But Sir Ambrose handled them as if they were treasures.

'I shouldn't wonder if Sir Stephen's own boys had played with these,' he said. 'I don't know, of course. But if so, then they have a certain value of their own. We'll have an expert down to look at them. Jones, you go down and see if any of them have survived the fall to the terrace, will you?'

'Right, sir!' And Jones began the descent to the flagged terrace. To him it seemed very doubtful that the marbles could have remained whole.

A sudden shout from Hiles brought him to a full-stop before he had gone very far.

'There's been a hole here, sir. It's all plastered up. I can feel it. You 'and me that chisel, Morgan, an' I'll chip it away. Like enough it's rotten with exposure and so on.'

Morgan handed up the chisel, and Sir Ambrose and the girls hung out of the window excitedly while the slow work went on, and Jones came back up the ladder, determined to be in at the death.

It took some time to chip away the old plaster sufficiently to allow Morgan to slip in his hand and feel about in the space behind the stair. But at length it was done, and they all waited breathlessly while he groped. Suddenly be uttered an exclamation.

'Something there, Morgan?' asked Sir Ambrose.

'Feels like it, sir. It's a wallet by the feel of it. I'll chip a bit more, and maybe it'll come out easier.'

''Ave the lever,' said Jones. ''Ere! I'll prise 'er up for you.'

But Morgan shook his head. 'That's no go. She's plastered as if she was meant to stand till Judgment Day. Can't lever *that* up nohow. You stand out o' the way, and I'll dig 'er out.'

Jones stepped back, and Morgan, one foot on the rung of the ladder, the other on a step, set to work in such grim earnest that he soon had quite a large piece chipped out. Then he laid down the chisel, and, to the amazement of the onlookers, lifted out the last piece of plaster quite easily, revealing a long crack about four inches across in most places; though at the outside end that widened to half a foot. Into this the young gardener easily thrust his hand, bringing out a leather wallet, about eight inches square. He felt again as Hiles handed the first find to Sir Ambrose, and produced a long, narrow box, bound with iron bands. It was only drawn out with some difficulty, for it was six inches deep, and Morgan had to manœuvre it so that it came out through the widest part of the crack.

'Is there anything else?' called Jesanne.

Morgan felt about. Then he drew out a long length of leather, black with age, and what was plainly recognisable as a dog-collar. The girls gave shrieks when they saw it.

'The dog-collar and leash Stephen missed! It tells in the Journall how they vanished one day,' exclaimed Sir Ambrose. 'I suppose one of the children must have hidden them and then been afraid to tell.'

'Where does that come?' asked Jesanne with interest. 'I don't remember seeing it.'

'Oh, it was some time after the expected raid by the Parliamentarians. If you remind me, I'll show you later. Now let us look at this.'

'There's a bundle here, sir,' put in Morgan, who had been rooting about in the crevice. 'And these 'ere, sir, too.'

He held up a small ring in which flashed a blue stone, and Sir Ambrose gave an exclamation. 'Loveday Penwarne's ring! Now how did that get there?'

'The ring she lost that Stephen tells about?' asked Jesanne eagerly. 'Oh, how thrilling to find it after all these years! May I see it, please? Look, Lois!'

The girls looked at the ring. It was a slender circlet of gold, ending in two hands which clasped the stone—a sapphire which was small but flawless, and of a rich, deep blue. Inside the ring, words were engraved. Lois snatched up a botanical glass from the table near by and with its aid spelled them out.

'Our hands together cling,
So shall our love outlast this ring.'

'Yes; it was a posy ring,' said Sir Ambrose, taking it. 'It was her wedding-ring, and no one knew where it had gone. Here, Jesanne, you are her descendant. It is yours by right. Take care of it for the present. When I go into Wyesford, I'll take it to the jeweller's and have it cleaned up, and make sure that the stone is secure.'

'Oh, Cousin Ambrose!' Jesanne was breathless with delight.

'I suppose someone must have slipped it in—it wasn't likely to get there anyhow else,' he said. 'And now, let us examine our treasure-trove.'

It certainly *was* a treasure-trove. They found the old lists just as they had expected. The ink was faded, and the paper rotten with age; but the stout leather wallet in which they had been enclosed had preserved them from complete destruction. There was a little bundle of letters which Nicholas had evidently contrived to get to the brother who had believed in him; and a quaint old missal with 'Nicholas Gellibrand his booke, from his tender mother' written on the fly-leaf. The bundle contained the little statuette of the Blessed Virgin—a lovely thing when it was cleaned and put in order—possibly the work of Benvenuto Cellini, the great silversmith. The tiny crown on the head flashed with small gems, and the Baby Christ wore a girdle of seed-rubies. The rosary was a very simple affair of silver beads; and the reliquary was of finest enamel set with black pearls and containing a shred of cloth.

As for the plan of the Dragon House, that gave them a whole evening's occupation in comparing it with the present building, and they were amazed to learn how much had been added to the original structure since that time. They spent one evening in the following week over it, helped by Miss Mercier, who was quite as interested in the find as even Jesanne and Lois could have wished.

The next excitement was the departure of the governess at the end of the week, for she would need all the time to prepare for her wedding, which had been put forward to a date in April, as her bridegroom had received an invitation to represent his hospital at a congress of doctors in America, and must leave for the United States early in May.

After that Lois and Jesanne settled down to a brief holiday, for Sir Ambrose assured them that they must have another governess as soon as he could find her. But before she appeared, yet another event took place.

He had driven into Wyesford in the morning, leaving his little cousin and her friend to amuse themselves at the cottage with the dogs and Little Tommy, and promising to return in time for lunch, together with a visitor. He was very mysterious about this visitor, refusing to say who it was, but assuring the girls that they would be very pleased when they knew all about it. He didn't even tell them if it was a lady or gentleman he was expecting, so they were wild with excitement.

And, as if that were not enough, Lois had been told that morning that June was to bring her a little new cousin, and had been permitted to pass the news on to Jesanne, though nobody else was to know for the present.

'I do hope it's a little girl cousin!' she said to Jesanne when they were discussing the news after Sir Ambrose had left.

'Why?' asked Jesanne, who was deeply interested.

'Because I think it'll help to make up to Auntie for little Edris. She's never said much to me, of course; but I can see how she's grieved for her.'

'Perhaps it'll be *both*,' suggested Jesanne hopefully. 'Wouldn't that be nice—twins? I'd love twins myself.'

Lois pealed with laughter. 'What an idea! But it's true enough. Both would mean the girl to make up for Edris, and the boy to be an extra. Oh, Jesanne, I think it's a lovely suggestion, and I do hope you are right.'

And, to anticipate a little, both it turned out to be, and great was Jesanne's triumph when she heard it.

However, that was all in the future. For the present the two girls decided to fill in the time by a good romp with the dogs, including Beowulf, and not forgetting Little Tommy, who kept the canines in judicious awe of his sharp claws. They raced about, all getting wilder and wilder, and shrieking, barking, and—on the part of Little Tommy—occasionally swearing.

Finally, just as Sanchia had chased her small playfellow up a tree round which all the dogs sat smiling, while Tommy told them what he thought of them in unprintable language, there came the sound of the car stopping, and Lois and Jesanne turned round.

Yes; there it was, and Sir Ambrose was helping out someone at

231

sight of whom Jesanne uttered a wild screech and then tore over the turf, her plaits flapping madly behind her, her eyes blazing with delight, and her cheeks pink with pleasure. Lois followed her at a more sober rate, and came up to the little group just as Jesanne with a final hug released the visitor.

'Lois! It's my Auntie Anne!' she cried 'It's Auntie Anne come to England! Did you ask her, Cousin Ambrose? Oh, you unmitigated *dear*!' And she would have flung herself on him with little heed for his crippled leg, had not Miss Mortimer caught her back.

'Steady, Jesanne! You mustn't fling your weight about like this! Let me look at you, child, for I haven't had a chance, so far.'

She held the girl at arm's length and surveyed her. Jesanne was untidy, rumpled, and her hair was tossed madly with her game. Her blouse had seen better days; there was a rip in one of her stockings; her light skirt was well smeared with green where she had slipped on the grass. But the colour in her cheeks, her sparkling eyes and round face were all signs of her well-being.

'I thought I was coming to nurse an invalid,' said Miss Mortimer as she released her niece, 'but I can only say that as a specimen of rude health you are the most shining example I have ever seen. Now let me speak to Lois, and then I must go and make myself fit to be seen.'

She greeted Lois affectionately, and established herself for ever with Sir Ambrose by petting the dogs and exclaiming over their beauty.

'Yes; your Aunt Anne is going to play hostess for you and me,' said Sir Ambrose that night when he and Jesanne were alone together for a few minutes. 'I sent for her when you had your fall, and she has consented to make her home with us for the next few years, and see to your governess and so on. It's rather beyond me, I think. But if God spares me, I propose to take you both back to New Zealand for a visit when you are eighteen, so you haven't said goodbye to your birthplace. And if He should call me before then, why, I hope you'll go just the same. But always remember that you are Gellibrand of the Dragon House, and that your rightful home must be here.'

'I shouldn't like it to be anywhere else now,' said Jesanne quickly. 'I'll always love New Zealand; but the Dragon House is Home.'

'More especially,' he added with a chuckle, 'since you've succeeded in solving our great mystery yourself, and found the Lost Staircase.'

CHRISTMAS AT THE DRAGON HOUSE

A short story by
Katherine Bruce

JESANNE GELLIBRAND, for the past month owner of the Dragon House and its surrounding estate, directed her pony, Rufa, along the path to Three Oaks. Sheltered by the centuries-old trees, she was out of the bitter wind of late December that had tossed her hair and blown sharp colour into her cheeks, and she flung back the hood of her cloak so that she could see in all directions. Her dark eyes traced the path up which she had come, Raphael's path, named for the third son of Balthazar Gellibrand, the man who had overseen the building of the Dragon House.

She had come here every day since Sir Ambrose died, and Rufa had become so used to the path that Jesanne had no need to use either the reins or her heels to direct the intelligent animal. The pony stopped to allow Jesanne to feast her eyes in every direction, taking in as much as she could of the land spread out beneath her. Not that she could see right to the far reaches of the estate, as the clouds were down, promising more bad weather. Rain had fallen the previous day and seemed likely to come on again before nightfall.

As her eyes picked out the splashes of colour that represented dwellings, Jesanne reminded herself that she meant to go to visit those of her tenants who would not be able to come to church on Sunday, to deliver the parcels of unrationed goods she had been distributing since the war began. The gardens belonging to those small houses were generally unable to provide enough to feed the large families who lived under the thatched roofs and so, soon after rationing had been introduced, Jesanne and Cousin Ambrose had decided to supply vegetables from the large garden beds that had been cut into the lawns around the Dragon House. Tenants were also permitted to scavenge for nuts and berries, as well as soapwort and other useful plants, on the estate, giving over a small portion of their finds to the great house and keeping the rest for themselves.

Before turning Rufa in the direction of the stables, Jesanne paused to look across to where the Dragon House stood and gave a cry of delight.

'The dragon of the Dragon House!' she exclaimed. 'At last, I've seen it again!'

It was one of the great mysteries of the grand mansion, and one to which her cousin had introduced her during her first Christmas in England: that, at certain times and in different lights, the house sometimes had the appearance of a great sleeping dragon. Jesanne had seen the phenomenon only twice in the three years since she came here. The first was on Christmas Eve, only a few months after her arrival, when Cousin Ambrose had begun introducing her to the many rites and rituals that existed within the Dragon House's long history. The second time had been not long before the outbreak of the terrible war that was gripping Europe and the world. And now Jesanne had seen it again.

'There's a legend, Jesanne, that only a true Gellibrand can see the likeness, and he but rarely,' Cousin Ambrose had told her on that first occasion.

Jesanne had been coming to this same place on the hillside, hoping to see the dragon again, ever since Cousin Ambrose had been laid in his grave beside his beloved children and grandchildren. She was not generally superstitious, but she had somehow felt that she would not properly come into her inheritance until she beheld the sleeping dragon again, and now, after so long, it had finally happened.

With a last look, Jesanne turned Rufa in the direction of the house, pulling her hood up so that she would not feel the sharp wind so plainly. As they headed for the house, she began to think about the forthcoming events of the Christmas week.

The previous evening had seen the visit by the Waits, and Jesanne had braced herself to serve the Christmas punch to every guest, and to receive the Rector's toast, as well as facing the strange loneliness of greeting each of the singers without Cousin Ambrose beside her. Even knowing that Auntie Anne was there did not lessen the burden Jesanne had felt settle on her since the dreadful day when the Dragon House had become her property.

She had trembled lest she spoke the words incorrectly, having spent hours studying them in the great Journall that lived in the library and told the house's story. Jesanne had felt very small and insignificant when the time came for her to begin recording the history of her own era in this leather-bound book. Still, she would not let herself shirk what she saw as her duty. It seemed to her that she owed it to Cousin Ambrose and to all the other owners of the Dragon House, as well as to those tenants who had grown up with them, to fulfil her part in the rituals and traditions of her home.

This evening Jesanne would take over the Dragon House Ritual for the first time, and she felt her nervousness grow at the thought of having to walk alone through the silent, empty house. Tomorrow she must set up the Christmas Story figures, and there would be the Basket in the evening, although it was a much smaller matter now that so many of the household had gone away to serve the nation.

The stables, as she came up to them, stood silent and empty.

She sighed sadly as she dismounted and led Rufa into her stall, remembering when this building, like all of them at the Dragon House, had been loud and busy. But then war had begun and the government had called for horses.

'But you didn't let them take you, did you, old thing,' she said aloud to her pony as she removed the saddle. 'Behaved as badly as you ever did, prancing and bolting and acting like one possessed, so they wouldn't take you. Clever old girl, aren't you?'

As if in reply, Rufa whinnied and nudged her mistress with her nose, making Jesanne laugh as she began to groom her.

Jesanne hated to see the other empty stalls, and to remember when they had been filled by the horses who had worked the estate, but she knew that it was the emptiness of another building that would most have upset Cousin Ambrose. From the doorway of the stables, she could see the kennels, always such a source of pride to the Gellibrands, but now also empty. The government had called for Dogs for Defence almost two years earlier, and although it had taken another year for the animals to leave, they had gone at last, all but three, including Jesanne's own Sanchia. Cousin Ambrose had refused to give up entirely on the Dragon House breeding programme, so Donna had remained, along with a male called Major. They had duly produced a litter and, only a week before his death, Cousin Ambrose had outlined plans for future ventures and the possibility of getting in new dogs once the war was over.

After his death, Jesanne had done her best to keep everything running as before at the Dragon House, but the challenges associated with the breeding kennels had been more than she felt able to manage. With a heavy heart, she had sold the dogs and puppies to a nearby estate, to people she knew her cousin had respected. Jesanne vowed to herself that, once the war was over and life had returned to normal, she would see to it that the kennels were once more full to bursting with dogs, but for now, their emptiness was a great source of sadness.

The Dragon House's only remaining dog, Sanchia, appeared now, rushing up to Jesanne, acting much like the puppy she had been when her mistress had first owned her, although she was as well trained as any other dog who had lived at the Dragon House. Laughing, Jesanne pushed away her affectionate fawning and scratched her head.

'Silly girl,' she told Sanchia, who gazed up at her mistress adoringly.

'How that dog dotes on you,' said a new voice, and Lois Bennett, Jesanne's great chum, strolled into the stables. 'You're lucky I cleaned her up or you would have muddy footprints all over you. She found that mud-puddle behind the kennels and, after rolling in it, tried to go inside and find you. Spike was having none of that, of course, and told me to do what I could to improve matters. I'd just finished when Sanchia heard you coming back and tore off to find you.'

'Thanks, old thing.' Jesanne finished grooming Rufa and let her loose in the stall. 'Spike certainly wouldn't want to have to clean up after one of Sanchia's rampages, particularly when she only finished the cleaning last week in time for Christmas.'

'Not that any of the Waits would have noticed,' Lois laughed. 'They were only too pleased to have some of the cake and taste the contents of the wassail bowl.'

'Cook did her best with it,' Jesanne remarked, 'but I can't wait for rationing to be finished so that it tastes as good as it did that first Christmas I was here.'

'Yes, you told me about it,' agreed Lois, becoming more sombre. 'And at least Cook let us help this time. We shan't be able to do that if the war goes on and we are called up.'

'That won't happen until we've had those two years at school that Auntie Anne has promised us,' added Jesanne, slipping her arm through that of her friend. 'I'm jolly glad that's to come first. Perhaps all of this will be over by that time. Not that I don't want to do my bit for the War, but it will be so nice when things go back to the way they were. And your parents will be able to come home,' she added, giving her chum an affectionate squeeze.

Lois nodded, blinking hard, as the two girls, accompanied by the dog, came out into the stable-yard. They walked round the side of the great house and stopped to look over what had been the large, well-maintained front lawn until it was dug up for vegetables.

'It's so awfully quiet.' Jesanne sighed. 'The place is terribly empty now.'

'Perhaps you should offer all those empty rooms to some more refugees,' Lois laughed, her gloom lifting. 'Another lot might be more willing to stay than the first. Remember how they all moaned and shrieked about how lonely and far away it was here.'

'And all those awful night-time noises,' said Jesanne as they entered the Dragon House. 'Owls hooting and Sanchia barking. The poor things had no idea what to make of all the peace and quiet.'

'Ah, there you are!' Anne Mortimer came out into the hallway to greet the girls. 'Lois, will you give me a hand with tea? Cook and Spike are busy in the kitchen so I said we would take care of it ourselves today. Jesanne, you will just have time to feed Sanchia if you hurry.'

The girls fled to do as they had been told. Jesanne prepared the feed for her dog and left Sanchia to enjoy her meal.

Returning to the house, she washed her hands before coming into the dining room where the others were waiting for her to pour the tea.

'Oh, bother,' she declared suddenly as she sat down. 'I never finished that entry I was writing in the Journall this morning. Spike came to speak to me and I lost my train of thought. I meant to come back to it and never did.'

'Well, you won't have any time before the Ritual,' replied Auntie Anne as she offered a plate of sandwiches to her niece. 'Perhaps you will be able to find some time after dinner.'

'I hope so,' replied Jesanne, taking a sandwich and passing the plate to Lois. 'It's a terrible bore sometimes, but I do want to keep a good record for the sake of the long history of the Dragon House.'

'There are the reports you're writing for the National Trust, too,' her aunt reminded her. 'They are another very important record, and likely to be read by rather more people than will get a chance to see the Journall.'

'Golly, I never thought of it like that.' Jesanne stared at her aunt out of wide eyes. 'D'you mean to say that people will read through what I wrote in the same way as we read through the Journall a few years ago?'

'I would expect so.' Miss Mortimer poured herself more tea. She had to smile at the horror in the girl's eyes. 'Don't look so petrified, Jesanne. It won't be that bad. It's just something for you to keep in mind when you next put pen to paper—not that you will have time for that today,' she added as she glanced at the clock on the mantel. 'When we finish here, you will have to prepare for the Ritual. Spike is going to help me clear so that Lois can help you dress.'

The girls hurried through the rest of the meal. Once they were allowed to leave the table, they made their way upstairs to Jesanne's bedroom. The dark-blue robe of the Ritual was already lying on the bed when they entered. Jesanne, as she always did, caught her breath at the sight of it.

It was delicate work to ease the fragile garment over Jesanne's head once she had divested herself of her other clothes. Four years ago, when she had first donned this robe, it had hung long and loose about her, but Jesanne had grown over that time and now it fitted much better. The red robe worn by the master of the house would have swamped her, but in any case she much preferred the blue.

'I'll let your hair out, shall I?' offered Lois, and when Jesanne agreed, her friend loosened the long, thick plaits of black hair that hung down her back.

The fillet of gold that matched the fringe of the blue robe was tied round Jesanne's head, keeping her hair out of her eyes, and then the girl slid her feet into the matching gold slippers that waited by the bed.

'Thank you, Lois,' she said to her chum. 'You can go down and join the others now.'

Lois smiled at Jesanne and left the room. Once she was alone, Jesanne turned to look at herself in the long mirror that stood in one corner. Her hand clutched the robe, but she saw that she no longer had to fear tripping over it, as she had done in previous years, for the gold fringe barely reached her ankles now.

Sighing at the remembrance of the other occasions on which she had worn this, Jesanne turned to the door and made her way out of the room before descending the staircase to the silent rooms below.

Her eyes turned to the spot where Cousin Ambrose had always waited for her, dressed in his own robe of rich red, but the place was empty now and Jesanne was forced to blink tears out of her eyes as grief struck her again.

A furry head nudged her and she looked down to find Sanchia standing beside her, the dog sensing that her mistress was upset and doing what she could to comfort her.

Jesanne bent down to hug her and then straightened and picked up the ancient horn lantern that stood, burning with a low light, in the centre of the floor. For a moment she studied it, ensuring that the candle inside was in no danger of blowing out, then looked down at the dog, who was still standing close beside her.

'Come, Sanchia,' she said in a voice that trembled slightly, and led the way down to the kitchens.

The rooms, as always for the Ritual, were dark apart from the light cast by the great fireplace. Somehow the empty room was more comforting than otherwise.

'Is anyone there?' she called, forcing herself to speak steadily, her voice sounding strangely loud in the silence space as she spoke the rest of the ancient words.

There was no answer, and Jesanne had not expected one. Still, she had made a beginning and she could almost have imagined that Cousin Ambrose was beside her again as she walked back into the main rooms of the house, visiting them one by one, repeating the same words. Sanchia's feet padded softly beside her, her playfulness temporarily absent, as if she recognised the importance and long history of the act they were now performing.

Room after room saw Jesanne make the same pronouncement, and each time she spoke the words aloud, she could feel herself becoming more confident. Her voice ceased to shake and she could give greater weight to the ancient message. She could even wonder, for the first time, what she would do if someone stepped forward to answer her summons.

'We would welcome them to our home, child, just as the Ritual insists,' Cousin Ambrose had told her when she had asked him that question several days after her first Christmas at the Dragon House. 'We would feed and clothe them if necessary, and we would treat them as honoured guests.'

The final room of the house was the chapel, and Jesanne struggled briefly with the key in the old, stiff lock before finally managing to turn it. Just in time, she remembered that here the words were different, that she must offer rest and sanctuary in this sacred space 'in the Name of Christ Who was once denied a resting-place save amongst the cattle, but who is now the King of Heaven, throned and crowned with glory'.

Thankful that she had not forgotten, Jesanne let herself and Sanchia out of the long, narrow room. They had now reached the top-most storey of the great house and so there were several flights of stairs to descend before they returned to the hall, and just in time. Even as Jesanne came down the final few stairs, the candle in her horn lantern spluttered and died, leaving the great space lit only by the second, fresh lantern that had been placed on the floor during her absence.

With a sigh of relief that she had not found herself in darkness in the chapel or one of the other rooms, Jesanne put the extinguished lamp on the floor where she had found it and turned to pick up the furred cloak that had been draped over the banister railing. It was a heavy garment, designed to keep out the icy December winds, and Jesanne was tired now, but she managed to drape it round herself after a fashion.

Picking up the lighted blackout lantern, Jesanne walked to the front door and opened it, and began making her way round the great house. As she moved along the terrace, she called again and again, trying to make sure her voice carried as her cousin's always had, when he called for anyone who might need comfort or shelter to find it at the Dragon House. Past the darkened windows she went, windows that led into rooms where she had already spoken this evening. Past the door that led into the great kitchens where she had offered the ancient invitation. Past the remains of the old stone staircase that had only been uncovered less than four years earlier.

At length, Jesanne and Sanchia came back round to the front of the great house, finding that the huge doors stood open to welcome them back inside. The heavy blackout curtains obscured the lights, which in former years had traditionally shone from the windows and doors at this point in the Ritual. Now, as for the past three Christmases, the hallway was perforce in darkness. However, when the servants ushered Jesanne into the drawing-room, she found that here the lights were lit. Totton took the lamp from her hand and extinguished the candle while Spike took care of the great cloak and then urged her upstairs.

Auntie Anne and Lois were waiting for her in her bedroom, and helped her to remove the precious robe. Jesanne was thankful to put on her dressing gown. She sat down at the dressing-table and began to brush out her long, dark hair, ready to plait it again.

'You've done very well indeed, Jesanne,' said her aunt as she carefully laid the robe on the bed. 'I think it would be a good idea if you had a nap before dinner. Mr Jennings will be coming to take Lois home then, and I know you will want to see him.'

'All right, Auntie Anne,' agreed Jesanne, too weary to object.

Lois picked up the robe and sandals as Miss Mortimer gathered the gown in her arms. At the doorway, the lady stopped and turned to smile at her niece. 'Your cousin would have been very proud of you this evening,' she said. 'So am I, child.'

Jesanne got into bed and curled herself up under the covers, thankful to realise, as she closed her eyes, that she had not disgraced herself or the Dragon House.

BIBLIOGRAPHY
(non-Chalet School books)

The La Rochelle series†:
Gerry Goes to School (1922)
A Head Girl's Difficulties (1923)
The Maids of La Rochelle (1924)
Seven Scamps (1927)
Heather Leaves School (1929)
Janie of La Rochelle (1932)
Janie Steps In (1953)

The Chudleigh Hold series:
Chudleigh Hold† (1954)
The Condor Crags Adventure (1954)
Top Secret (1955)

Fardingales (Associated title) (1950)
The Susannah Adventure (Associated title) (1953)

A Thrilling Term at Janeways* (1927)
Caroline the Second* (1937)
The New House-Mistress (1928)
Judy the Guide (1928)
The Feud in the Fifth Remove (1932)
Carnation of the Upper Fourth (1934)
Monica Turns Up Trumps† (1936)
They Both Liked Dogs (1938)
The School by the River† (1930)
The Little Marie-José (1932)
Elizabeth the Gallant (1935)

The Little Missus (1942)
The Lost Staircase† (1946)
Lorna at Wynyards†+ (1947)
Stepsisters for Lorna†+ (1948)
Kennelmaid Nan (1953)
Nesta Steps Out (1954)
Beechy of the Harbour School (1955)
Leader in Spite of Herself (1956)
The School at Skelton Hall# (1962)
Trouble at Skelton Hall# (1963)
Bess on Her Own in Canada‡ (1951)
A Quintette in Queensland‡ (1951)
Sharlie's Kenya Diary‡ (1951)
Verena Visits New Zealand‡ (1951)
Jean of Storms (1996; available from Bettany Press. EBD's only adult novel, first serialised in *The Shields Gazette* in the 1930s)

† Chalet School connector
* Linked titles
+ Linked titles
# Linked titles
‡ Geography reader

Short Stories§:
'Carlotta To The Rescue'; published in *The Children's Circus Book* and in a pamphlet
'Jack's Revenge' by 'May Dyer'; published in *Sunday* in 1914
'The Robins Make Good'; published in Volume 57 of *The Girl's Own Annual*
'The Lady in the Yellow Gown'; published in *The Big Book For Girls* in 1925

'Rescue in the Snows'; published in *My Favourite Story*
'The House of Secrets'; published in *The Sceptre Annual For Girls* (shortened version of *Fardingales*)
'Cavalier Maid'; published in *The Second Coronet Book For Girls* (shortened version of *Elizabeth The Gallant*)

§ All but the last two stories were reprinted in *Elinor M Brent-Dyer's Short Stories* (Girls Gone By Publishers, 2005; out of print).

A complete list of the Chalet School series may be found in the GGBP editions of the Chalet School books and also at www.chaletschool.org.uk

Girls Gone By Publishers

Girls Gone By Publishers republish some of the most popular children's fiction from the 20th century, concentrating on those titles which are most sought after and difficult to find on the second-hand market. Our aim is to make them available at affordable prices, and to make ownership possible not only for existing collectors but also for new ones, so that the books continue to survive.

We also publish some new titles which fit into the genre, including our Chalet School fill-ins, all professionally edited. Authors on the GGBP fiction list include Helen Barber, Elinor Brent-Dyer, Katherine Bruce, Patricia Caldwell, Gwendoline Courtney, Monica Edwards, Adrianne Fitzpatrick, Antonia Forest, Lorna Hill, and Malcolm Saville.

We also publish non-fiction titles, currently Alison McCallum's *The Chalet School Encyclopaedia* in four volumes. The non-fiction books are in a larger format than our fiction, and they are lavishly illustrated in black and white.

For details of availability and when to order, see our website or write for a catalogue to GGBP, The Vicarage, Church Street, Coleford, Radstock, Somerset, BA3 5NG, UK

www.ggbp.co.uk
www.facebook.com/girlsgonebypublishers